Bricks

Extra Credit Books

Text: Paul Andersen

Drawings: Drew Stanley and Paul Andersen

ISBN 979-8-218-76828-7

First Edition, 2025.

This book builds on Melissa Price's work, *Brick Bonds*, an illustrated collection of bond patterns. Melissa's generous support made possible the expanded catalog of bonds included here.

Bricks

Paul Andersen

Extra Credit Books

2025

Contents

Introduction

People have been building with brick for a long time, mostly because it is convenient and durable. You can make a brick from mud, it is easy to pick up and place, and it will last a long time. Brickmaking was simplest in the beginning. Bricks were hand shaped from whatever earth was nearby and dried in the sun. Over time, production was refined. Firing bricks in kilns made them harder. Molds ensured uniform sizes and shapes. Mechanized production increased availability and reduced cost.

Brick design also improved, in both practical and daring examples. Brick was initially used for small houses and storage buildings. And its identity as an everyday material persisted, whether in the façade of a modest warehouse or in the hidden core of a Baroque church. More ambitious projects pushed the limits of engineering, form, and intricacy. Despite their small size, bricks have been used to build enormous structures. Among the most astounding examples are the 400' tall Jetavanaramaya stupa and the Hanging Gardens of Babylon, which sprawled across a terraced mountain made of solid brick. Other projects pushed brick's ornamental potential. In cultures as far flung as ancient Sumer and Victorian England, elaborate brick buildings were the pinnacle of architectural expression.

Many advances in brick construction connected visual sophistication to structural performance. For instance, as brick arches evolved, they took on a variety of elegant profiles that were also stronger. And bricklaying patterns became more flamboyant when they incorporated rotated bricks, which bonded multiple layers of brick to make a thicker wall. But in the past century, a 10,000 year tradition of using brick structurally petered out. Cheaper and stronger materials that could be better insulated took over. Mudbrick and concrete block have remained common, but they work differently. So, the demise of brick structure has made most of its technical innovations obsolete.

This book is a nostalgic compilation of fading knowledge from brick's best days. It is an attempt to enshrine brick with dignity, to capture the intelligence and beauty of the innumerable ways that it has been used. Before long, structural brick will probably disappear. Maybe some of its ingenuity can serve a different purpose.

Technical Standards

Face and Joint Names

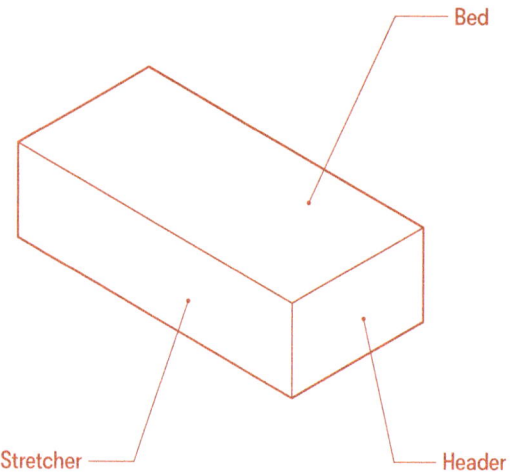

Bed

Stretcher

Header

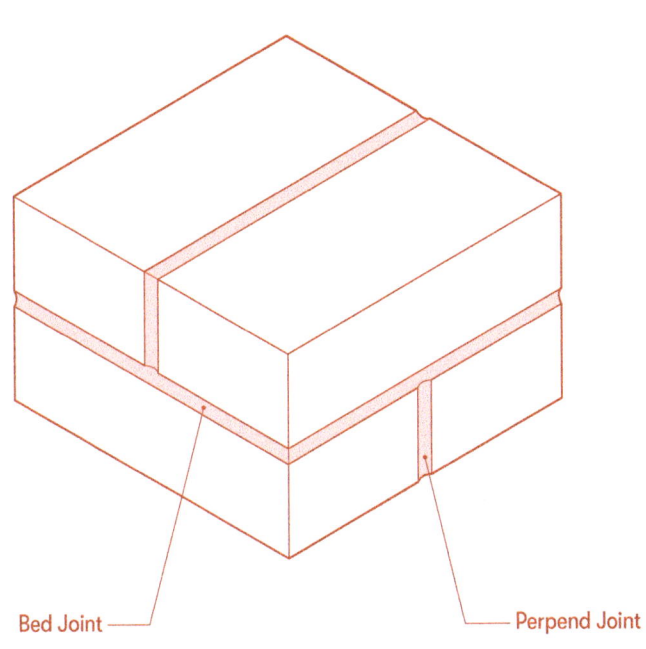

Bed Joint ———   ——— Perpend Joint

Orientations

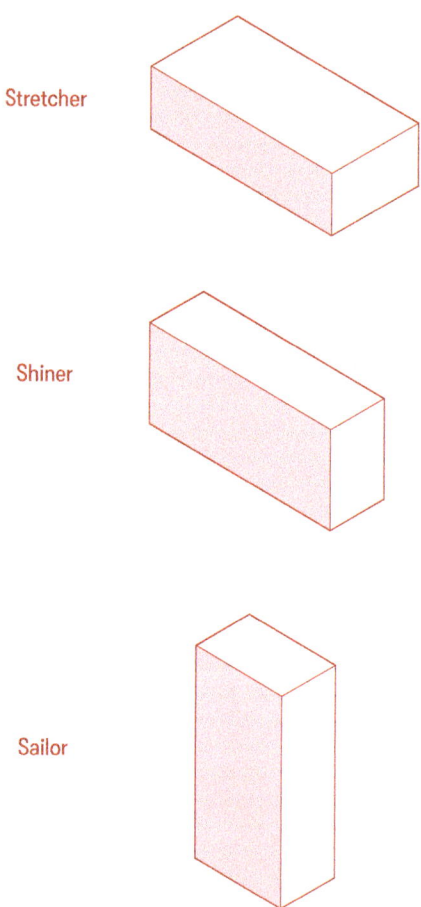

Stretcher

Shiner

Sailor

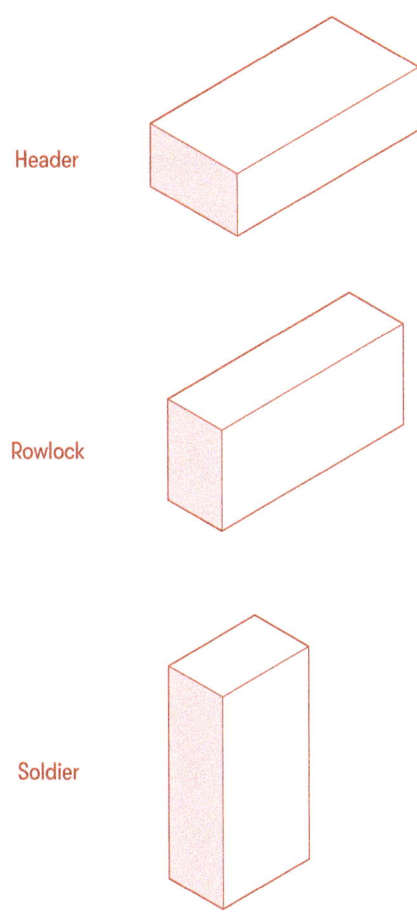

Header

Rowlock

Soldier

Forms

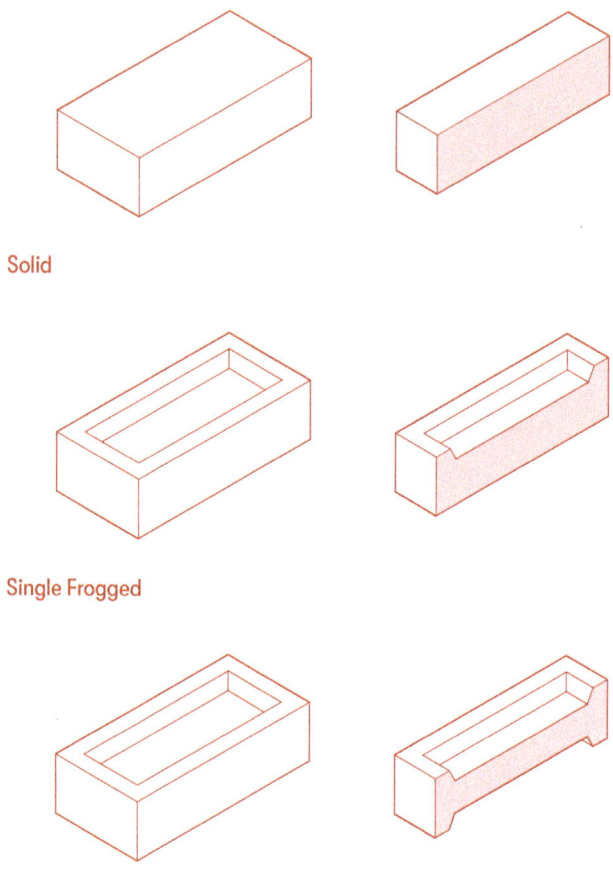

Solid

Single Frogged

Double Frogged

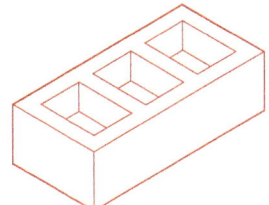
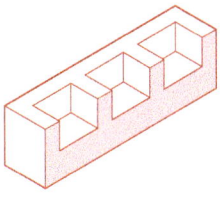

Cellular

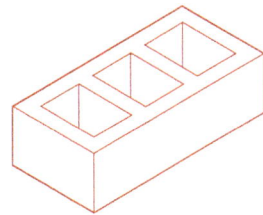
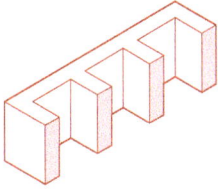

Perforated
(holes > 25% of volume)

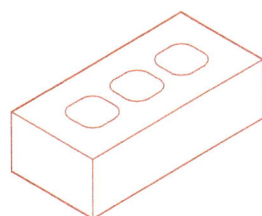
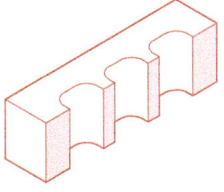

Hollow
(holes < 25% of volume)

Sizes

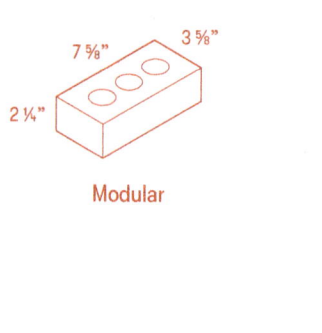

Modular

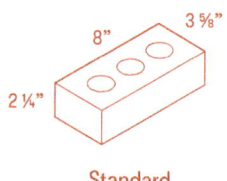

Standard

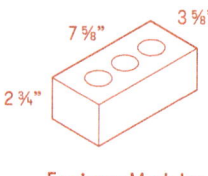

Engineer Modular

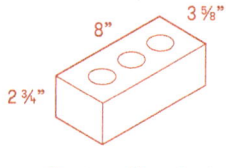

Engineer Standard

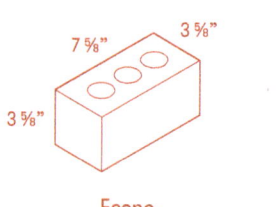

Econo

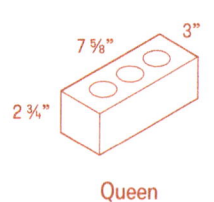

Queen

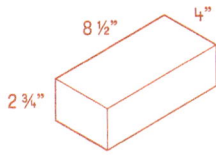

8 ½" 4"

2 ¾"

Handmade Oversize

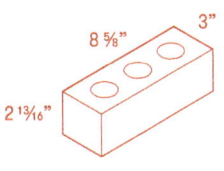

8 ⅝" 3"

2 ¹³⁄₁₆"

Builders' Special

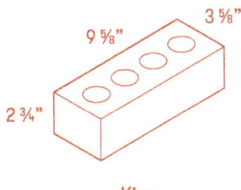

9 ⅝" 3 ⅝"

2 ¾"

King

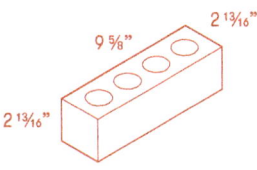

9 ⅝" 2 ¹³⁄₁₆"

2 ¹³⁄₁₆"

Engineer King

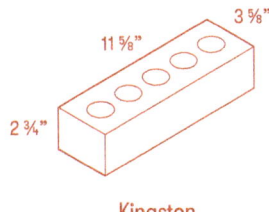

11 ⅝" 3 ⅝"

2 ¾"

Kingston

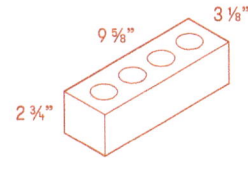

9 ⅝" 3 ⅛"

2 ¾"

King Narrow Bed

Sizes

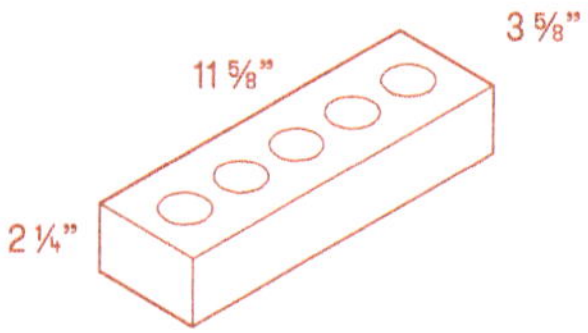
3 ⅝”
11 ⅝”
2 ¼”

Norman

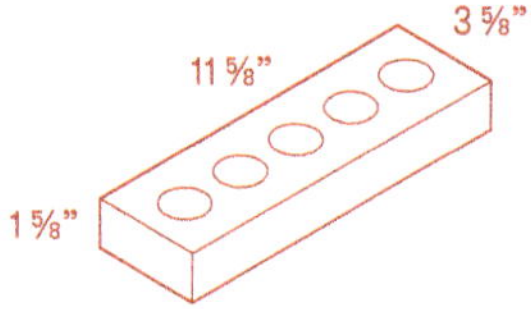
3 ⅝”
11 ⅝”
1 ⅝”

Roman

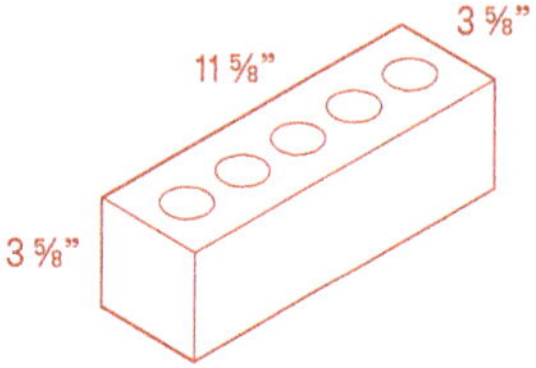
3 ⅝”
11 ⅝”
3 ⅝”

Utility

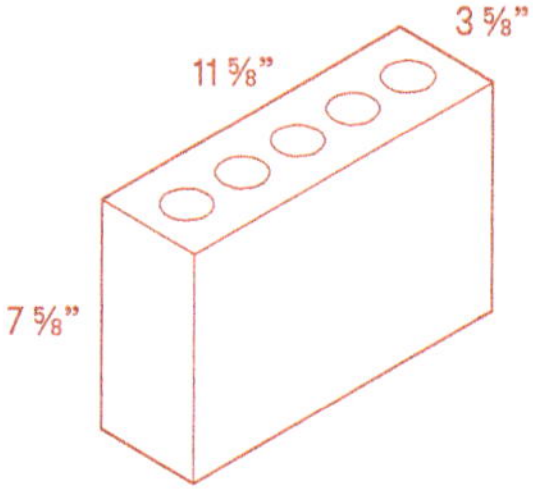
3 ⅝”
11 ⅝”
7 ⅝”

Double Utility

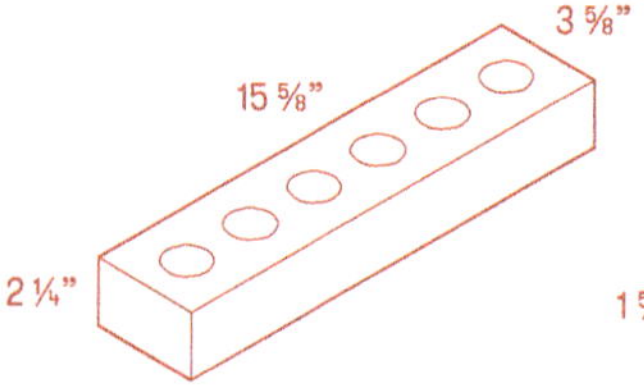
3 ⅝”
15 ⅝”
2 ¼”

Saxon

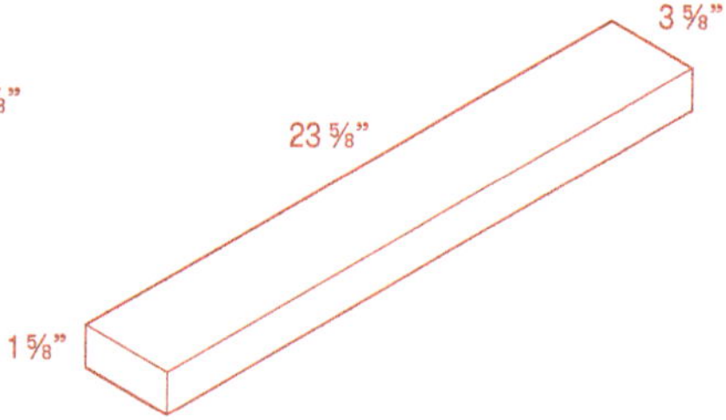
3 ⅝”
23 ⅝”
1 ⅝”

Roman Maximus

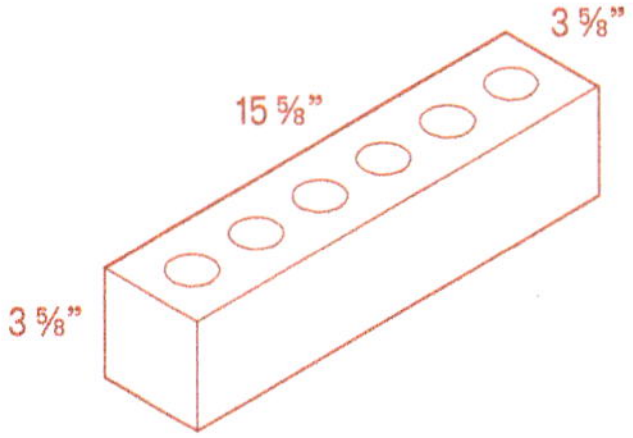
3 ⅝"
15 ⅝"
3 ⅝"

Titan

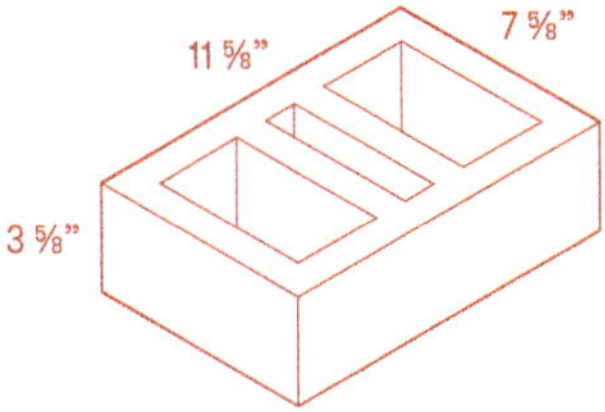
7 ⅝"
11 ⅝"
3 ⅝"

Regent

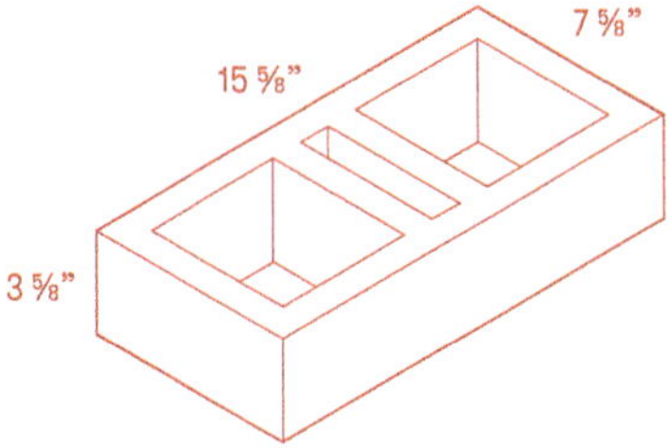
7 ⅝"
15 ⅝"
3 ⅝"

Titan Plus

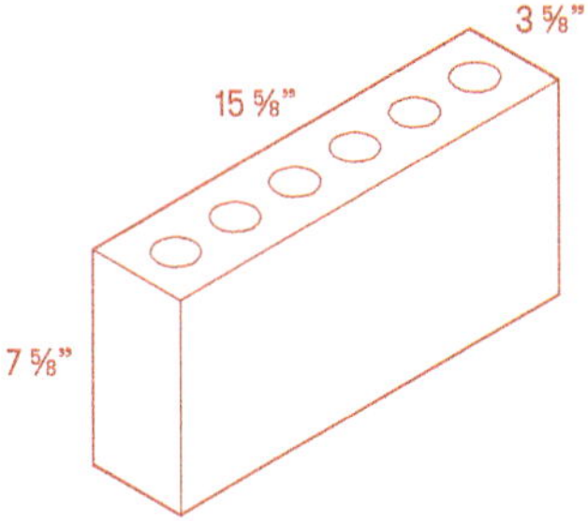
3 ⅝"
15 ⅝"
7 ⅝"

Double Titan

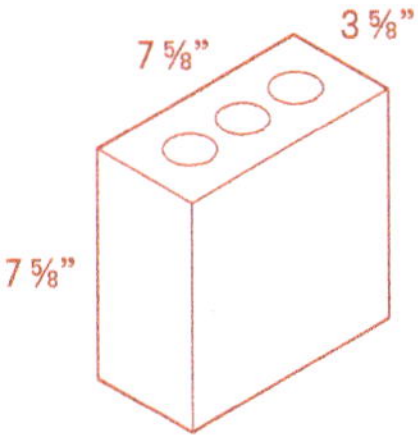
7 ⅝"
3 ⅝"
7 ⅝"

8-Square

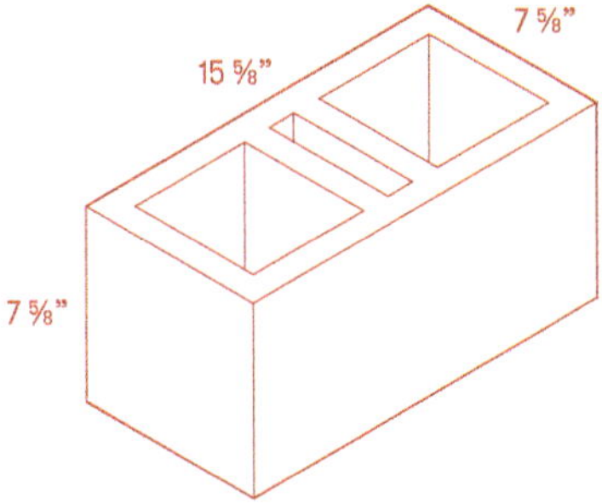
7 ⅝"
15 ⅝"
7 ⅝"

Double Titan Plus

Joint Types

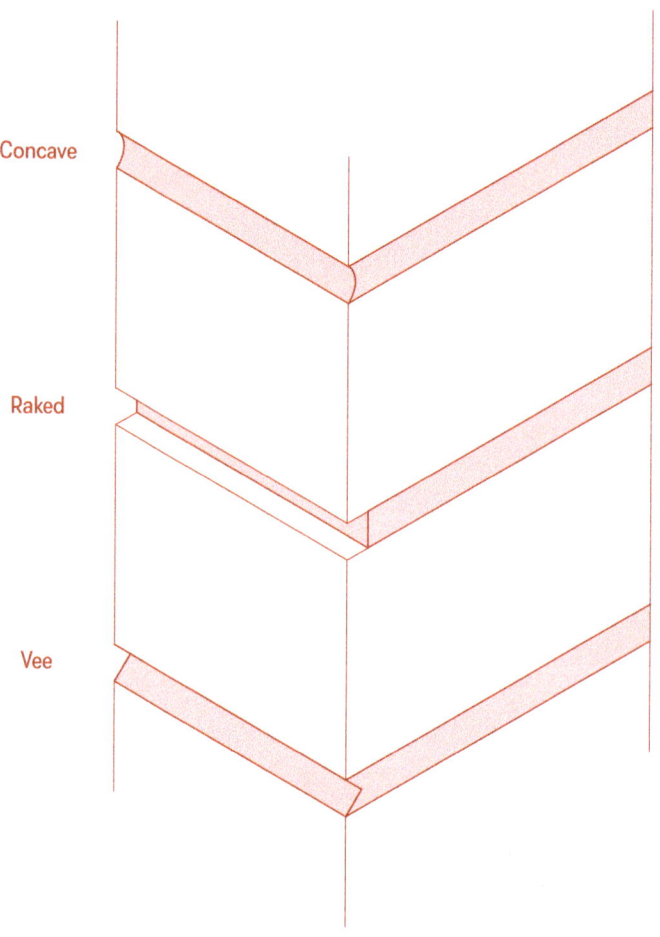

Concave

Raked

Vee

Weathered

Weatherstruck
and Cut

Overhand
Struck

Joint Types

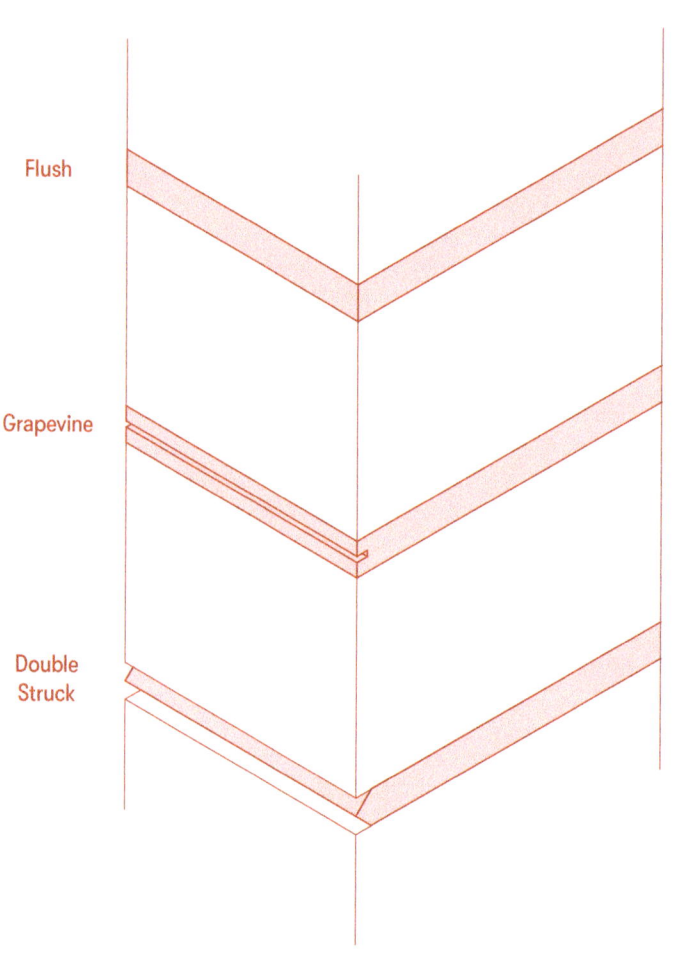

Flush

Grapevine

Double
Struck

Weeping

Beaded

Extruded

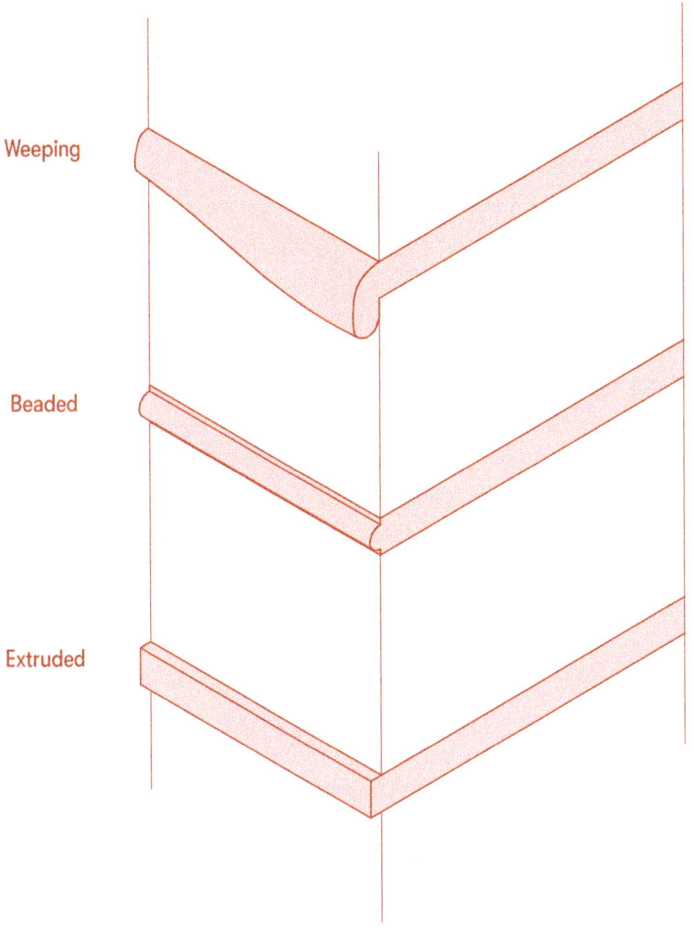

Layers

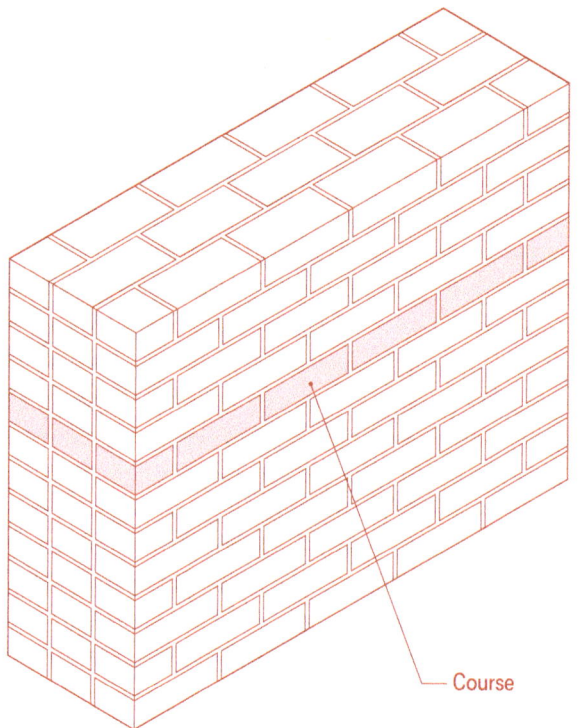

Course

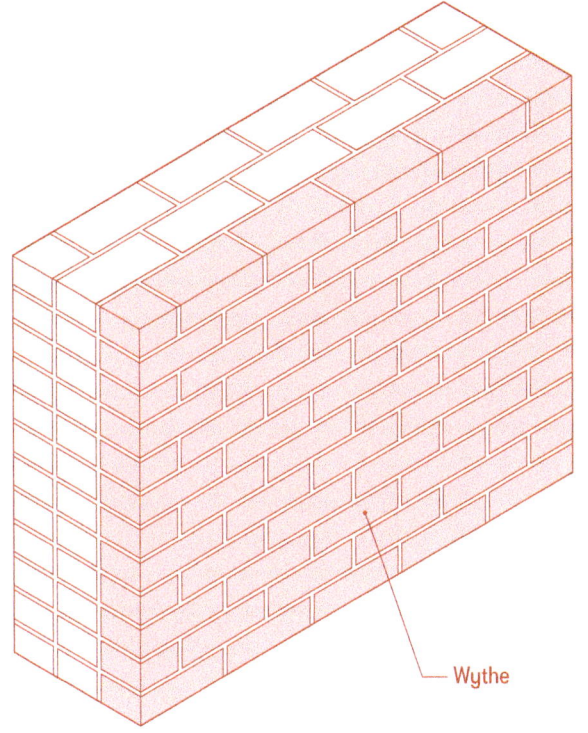

Wythe

Quoins and Cuts

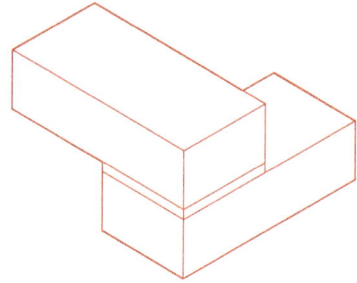

Quoin
(two adjacent vertical sides exposed)

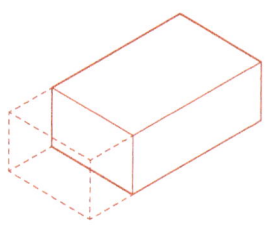

Three-Quarter Bat

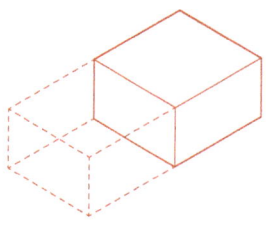

Half Bat

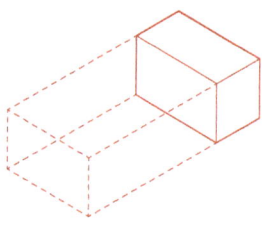

Quarter Bat

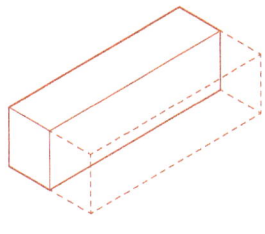

Queen Closer

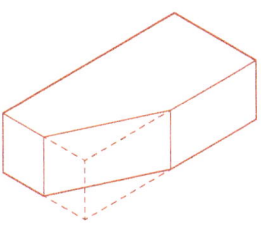

King Closer

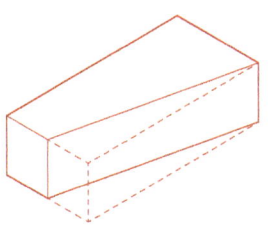

Beveled Closer

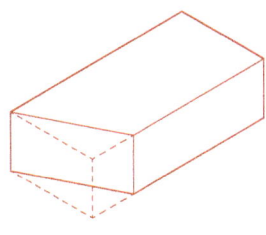

Mitered Closer

Quoins and Cuts

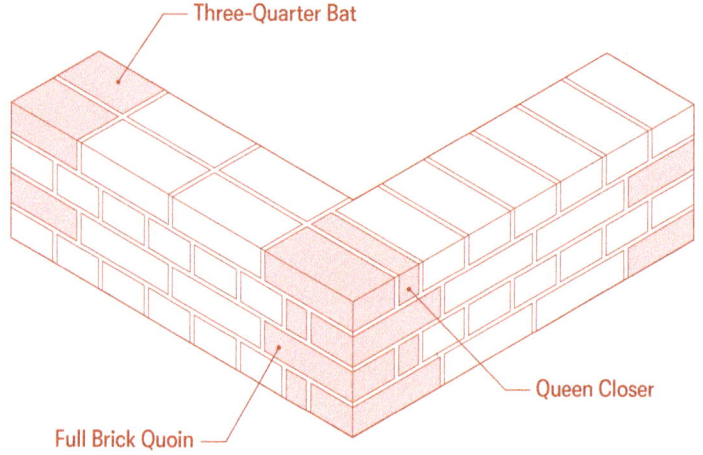

Three-Quarter Bat

Queen Closer

Full Brick Quoin

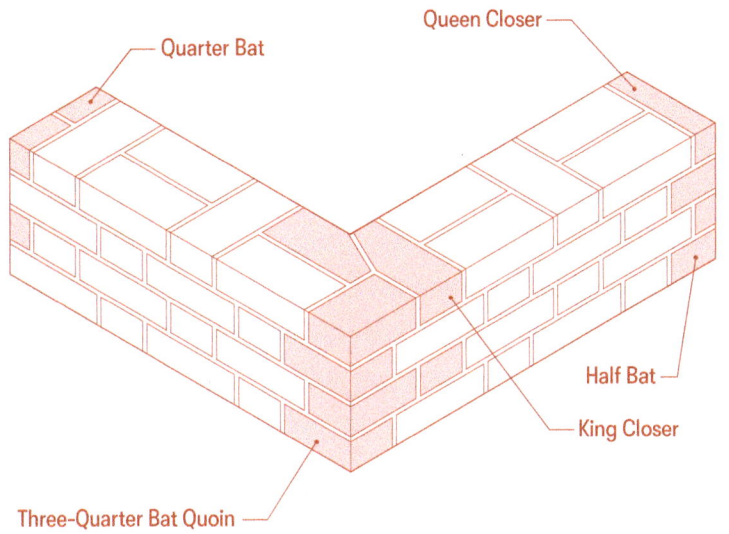

Quarter Bat

Queen Closer

Half Bat

King Closer

Three-Quarter Bat Quoin

English Bond

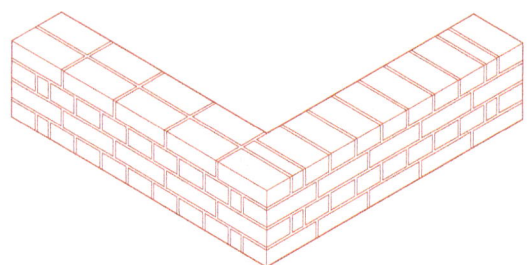

1 Unit Thick

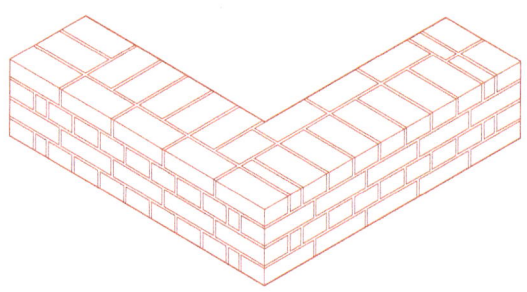

1.5 Units Thick

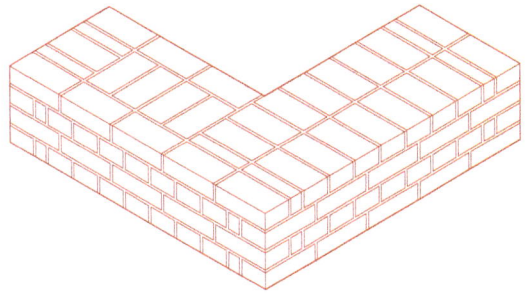

2 Units Thick

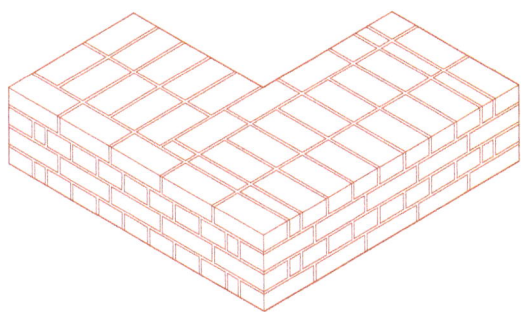

2.5 Units Thick

Flemish Bond

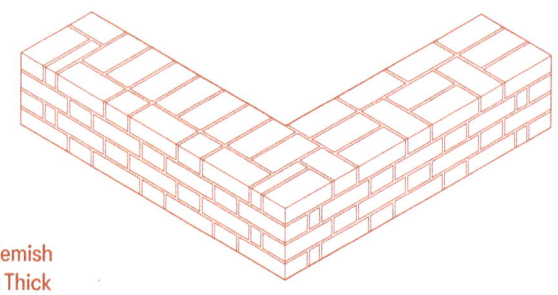

Single Flemish
1.5 Units Thick

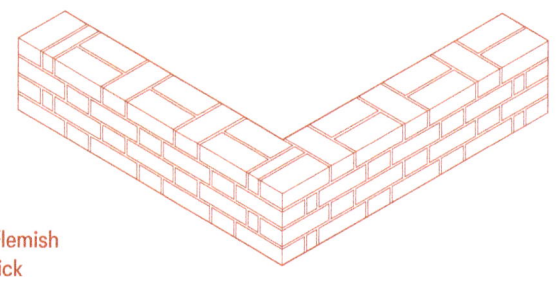

Double Flemish
1 Unit Thick

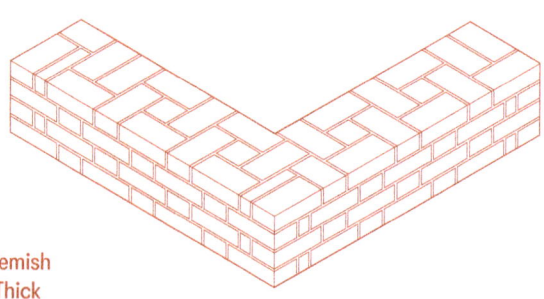

Double Flemish
1.5 Units Thick

Double Flemish
2 Units Thick

Double Flemish
2.5 Units Thick

Double Flemish
3 Units Thick

Hollow Wall Bonds

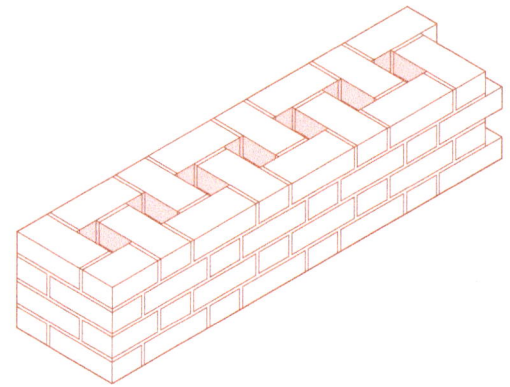

Quetta Bond

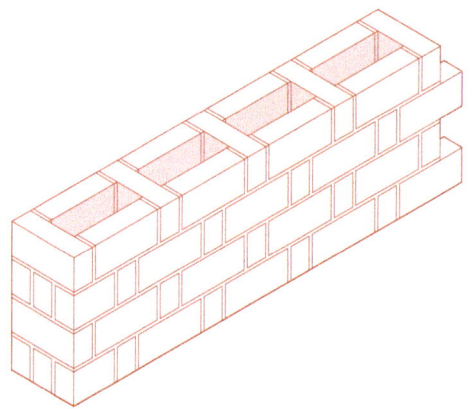

Rat Trap Bond

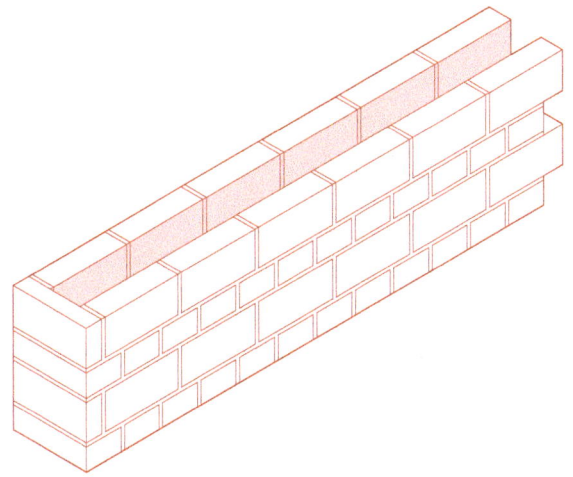

Dearne's Bond

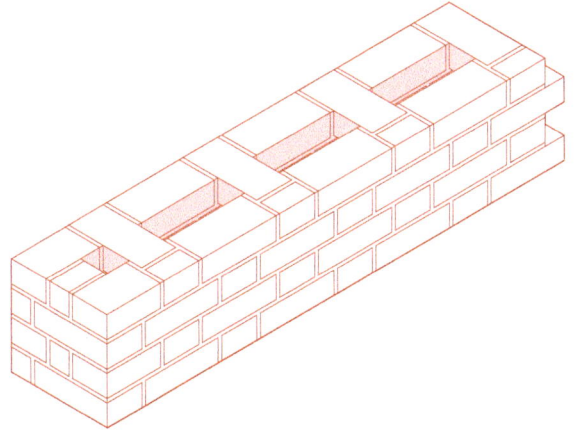

Loudon's Hollow Wall Bond

Special Shapes

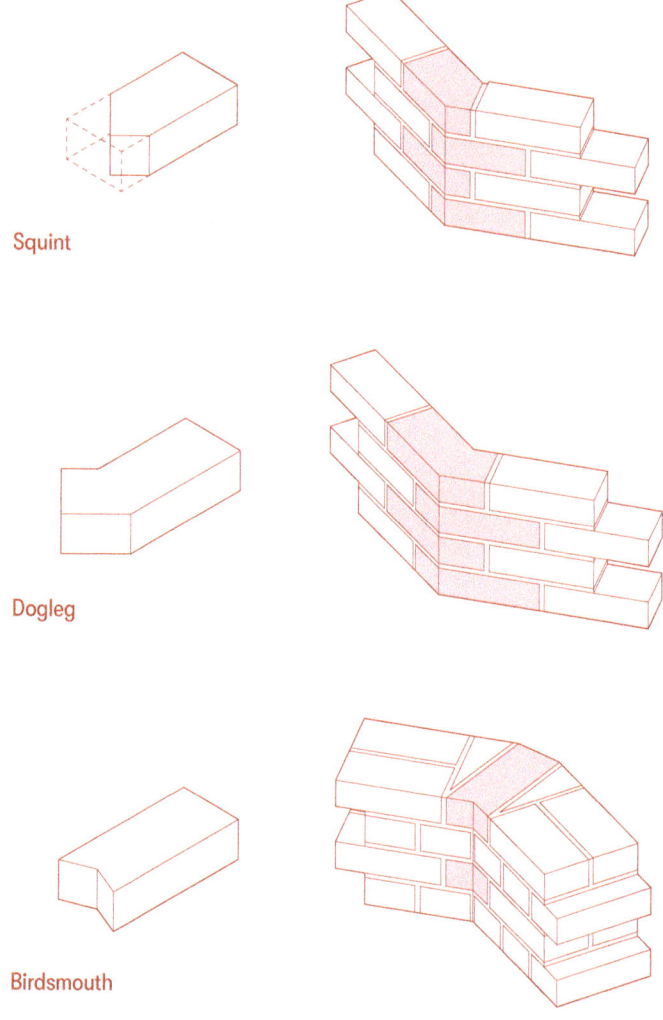

Squint

Dogleg

Birdsmouth

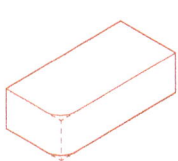

Bullnose

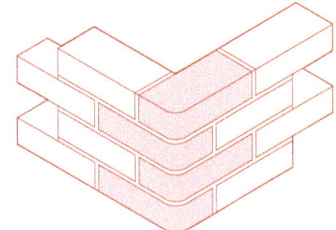

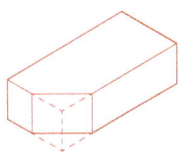

Cant

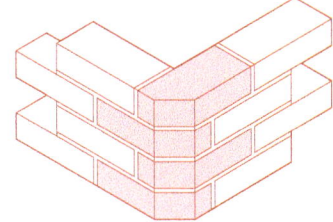

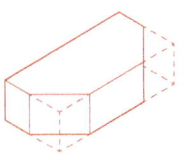

Double Cant

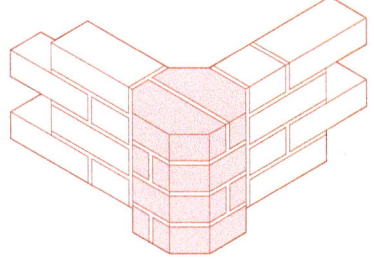

Special Shapes

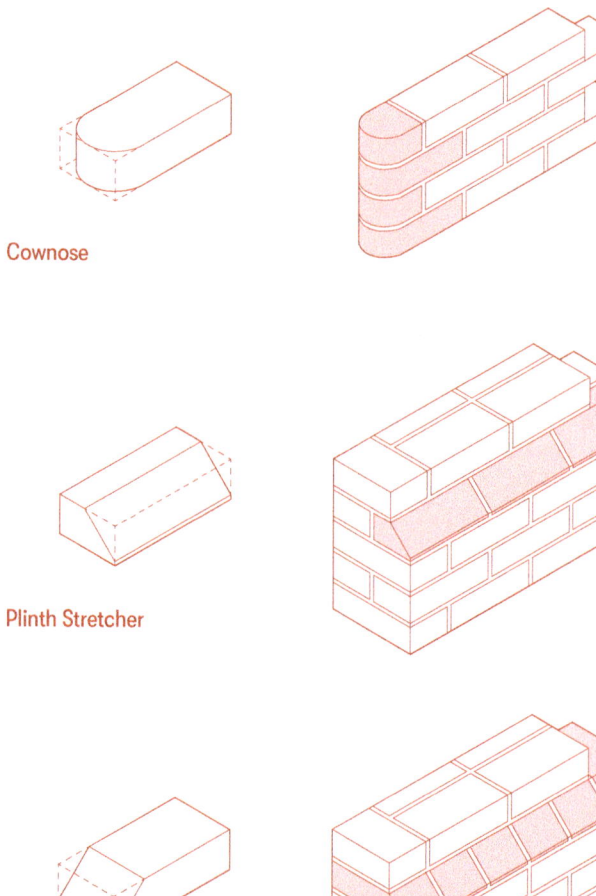

Cownose

Plinth Stretcher

Plinth Header

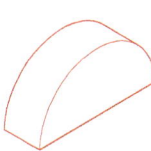

Half Round Capping

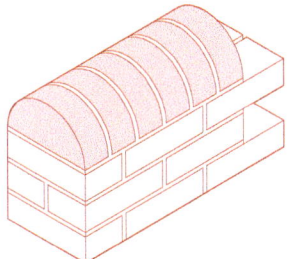

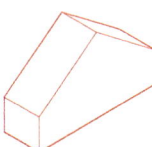

Saddleback Capping

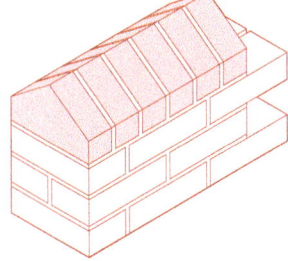

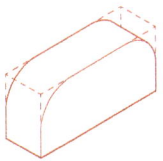

Double Bullnose Capping

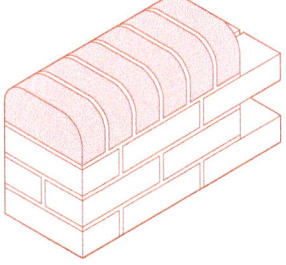

Decorative Features

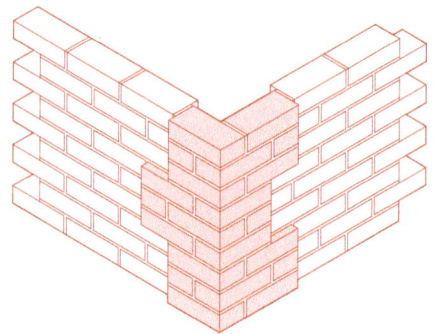

Rusticated Quoin

Circular Ramp

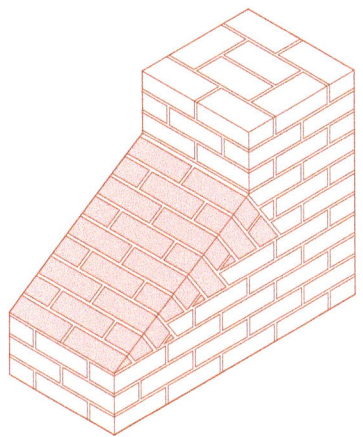

Tumbling In

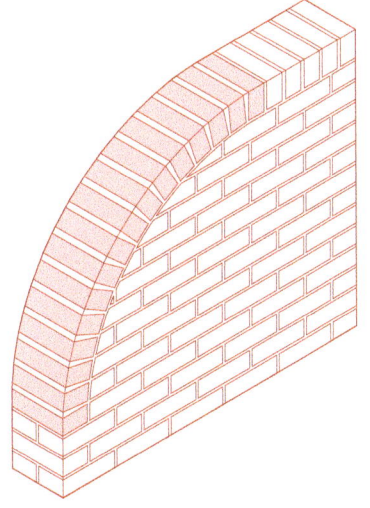

Quadrant

43

Decorative Features

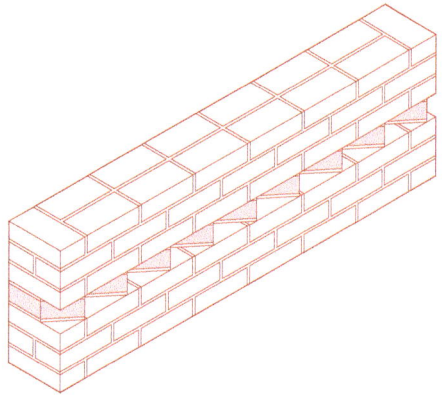

Dogtoothing

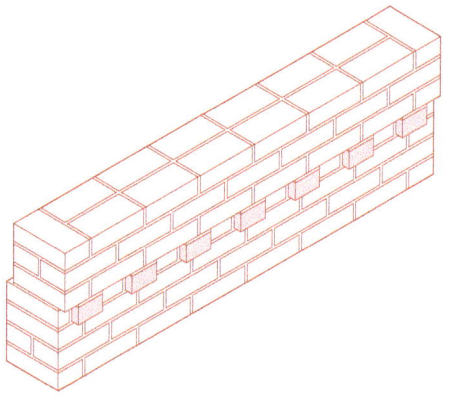

Dentil Course

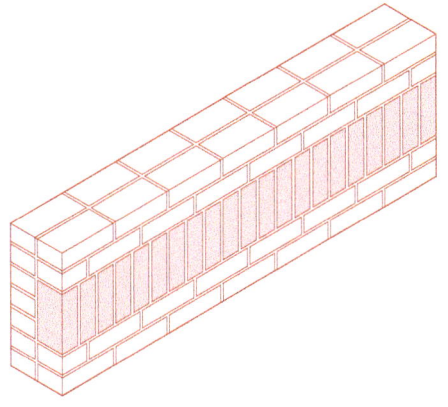

Soldier Course

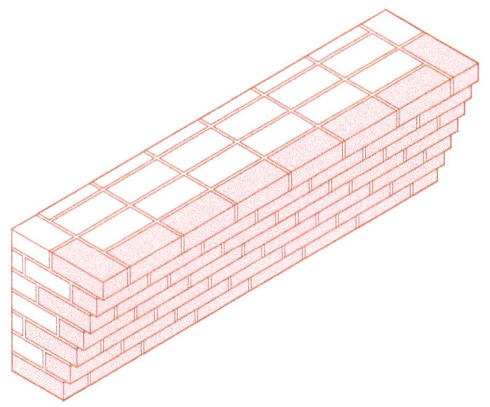

Corbelling

Decorative Panels

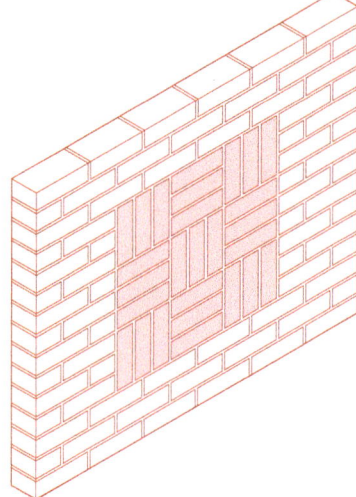

Basketweave

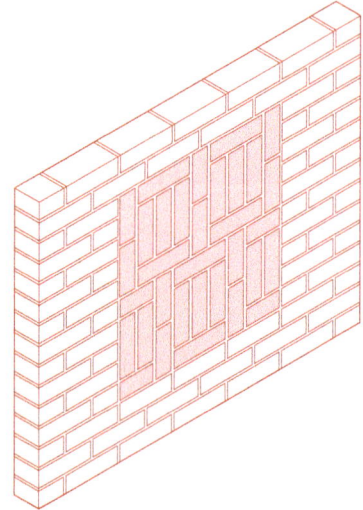

Boxed Basketweave

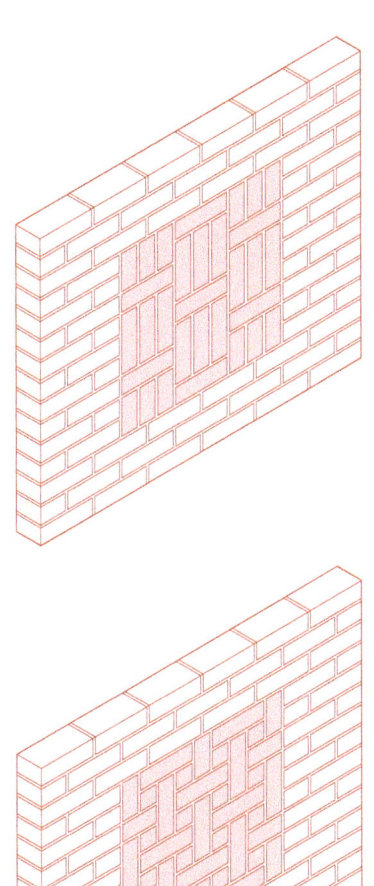

Single Basketweave

Victorian Weave

Decorative Panels

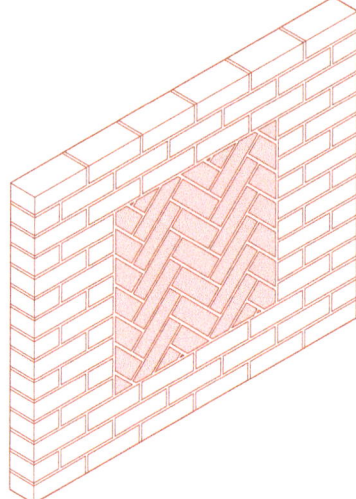

Herringbone

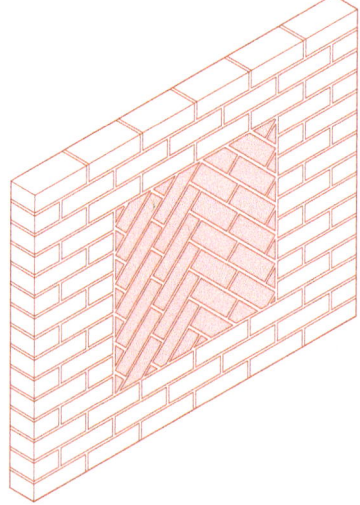

Chevron

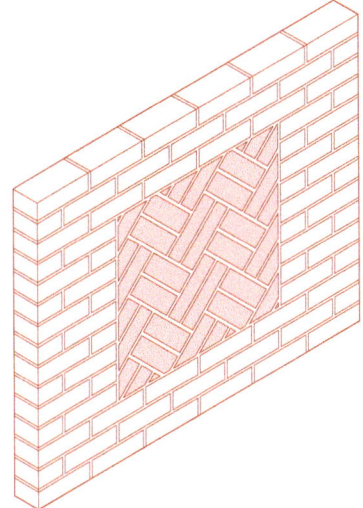

Double Herringbone

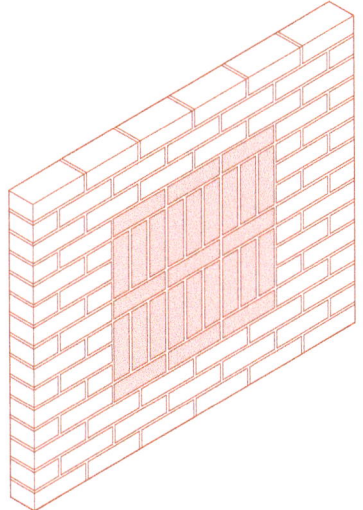

Running Stack

Arches

Terms

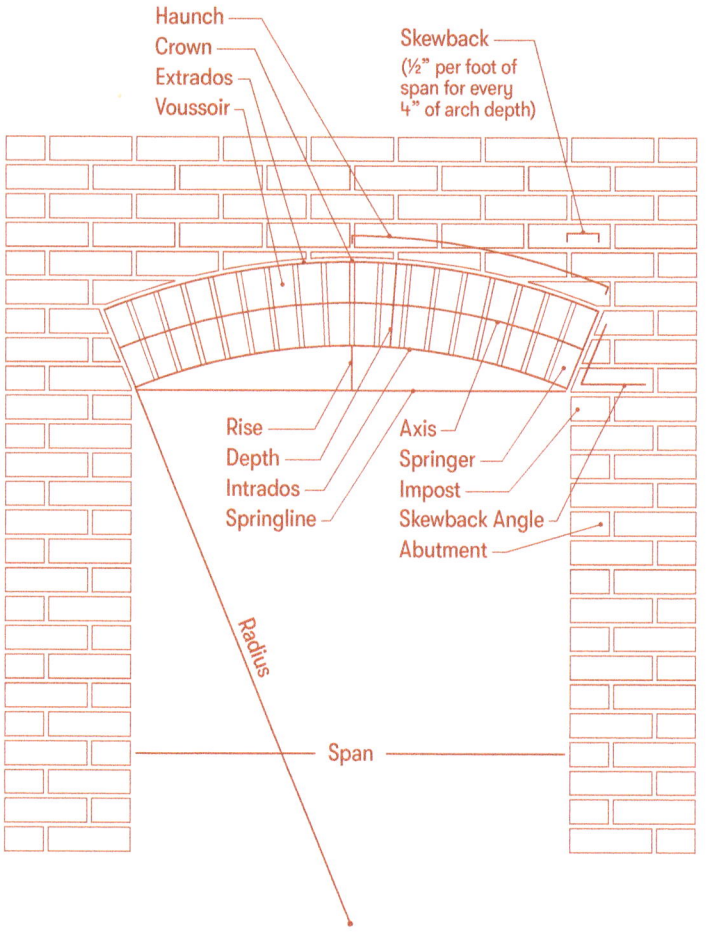

Haunch

Crown

Extrados

Voussoir

Skewback
(½" per foot of
span for every
4" of arch depth)

Rise

Depth

Intrados

Springline

Axis

Springer

Impost

Skewback Angle

Abutment

Radius

Span

Segmental

Bricks laid out so that outer edges are full width

Two Course

Three Course Rowlock

All bricks are gauged, or shaped from full bricks, except in a Rowlock Arch.

Gauged Jack

Dutch Jack

Pointed Segmental

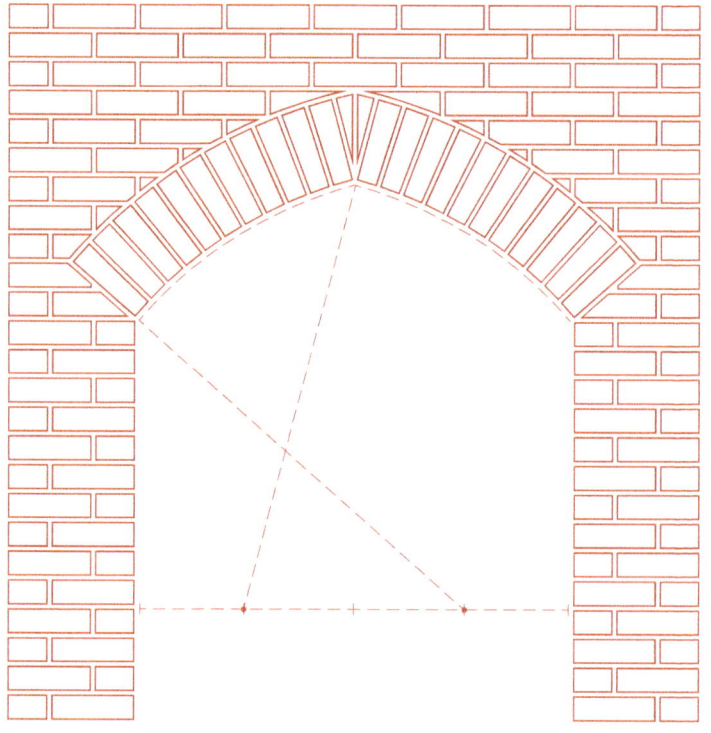

Gothic / Pointed

Drop Arch if the radius is less than the span.
Equilateral Arch if the radius equals the span.
Lancet Arch if the radius is greater than the span.

Roman

Florentine

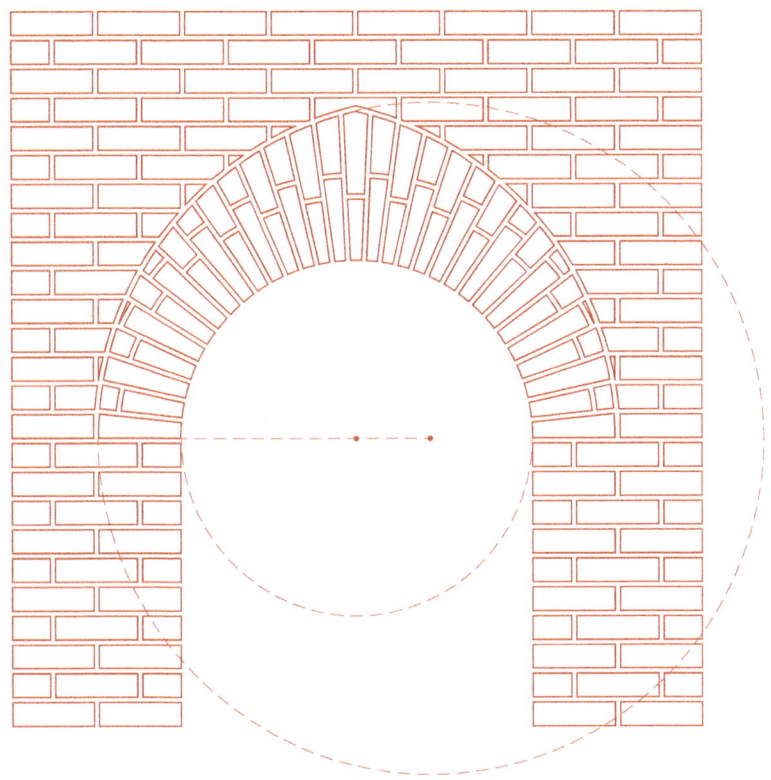

Fillet / Pseudo Three Centered

False Tudor / Pseudo Four Centered

Tudor / Four Centered

Ogee

Keel

Draped

Multi Draped

Inflexed

Shouldered

Trefoil

Pointed Trefoil

Cinquefoil

Pointed Cinquefoil

Multifoil

Pointed Multifoil

Tapered Horseshoe

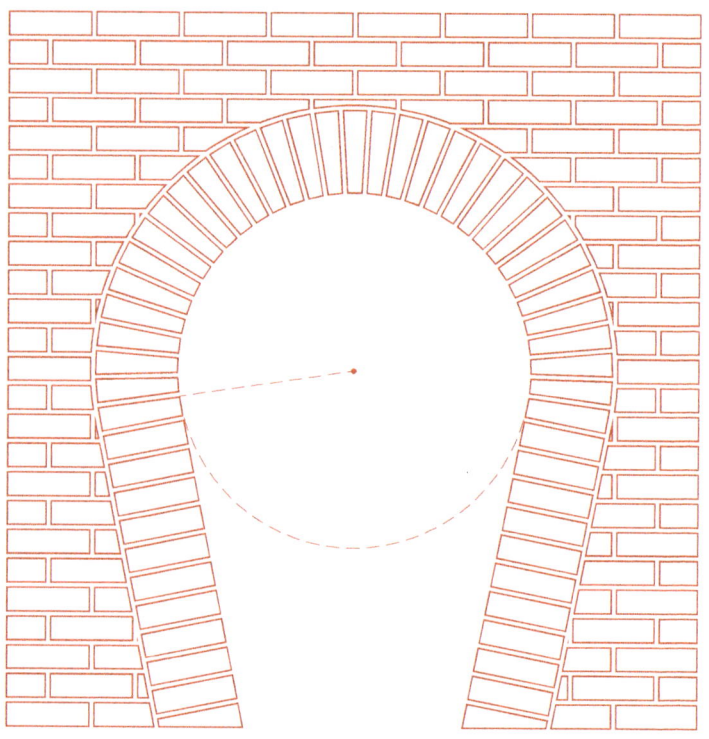

Keyhole / Horseshoe

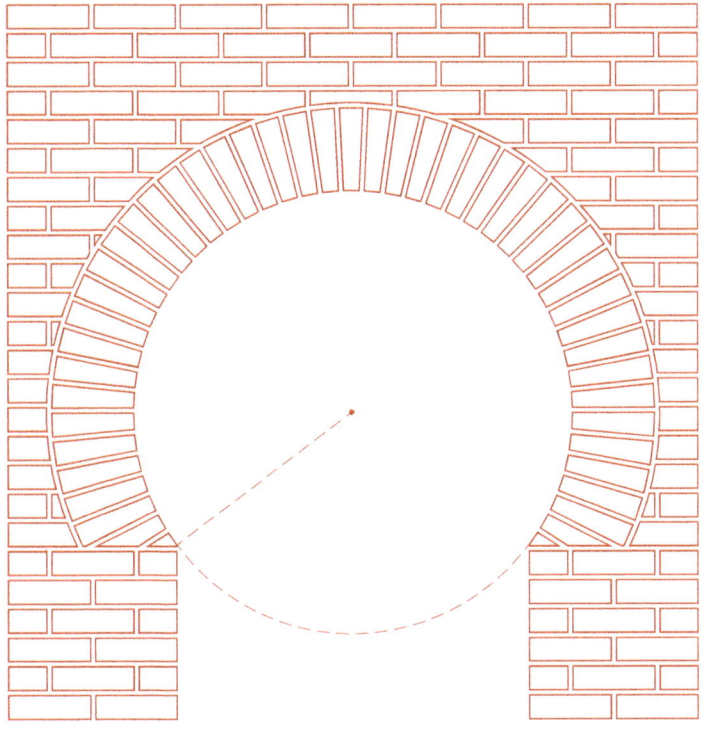

Double Keyhole

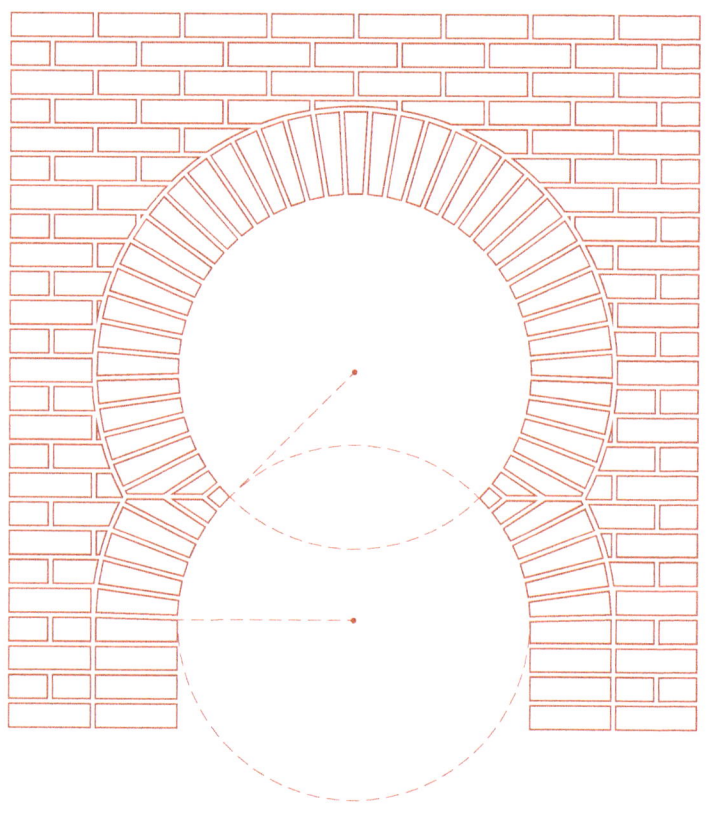

Pointed Keyhole

Tudor Keyhole

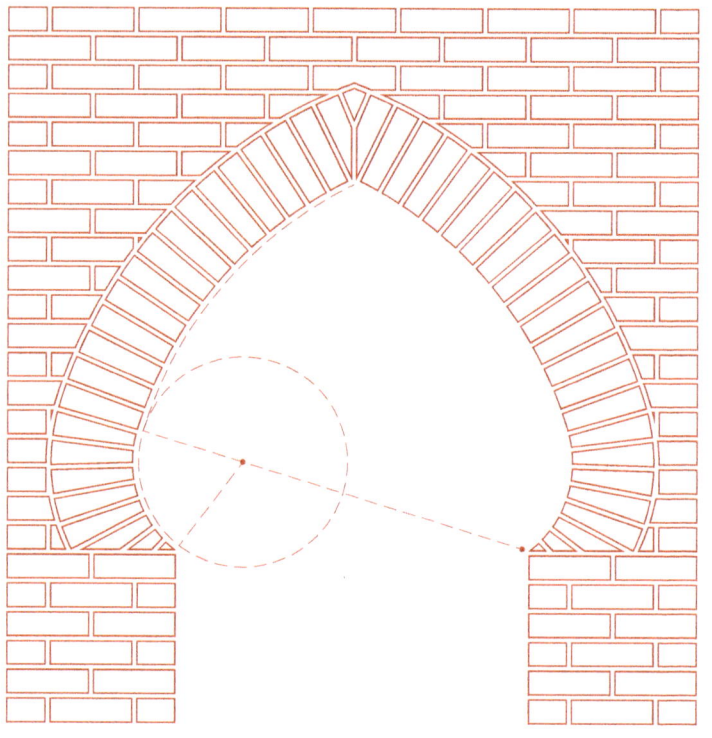

Parabolic

Rampant

Pointed Rampant

Quadrant

Triangular / Pediment / Miter

Bonds

Stack

Block

Running / Stretcher

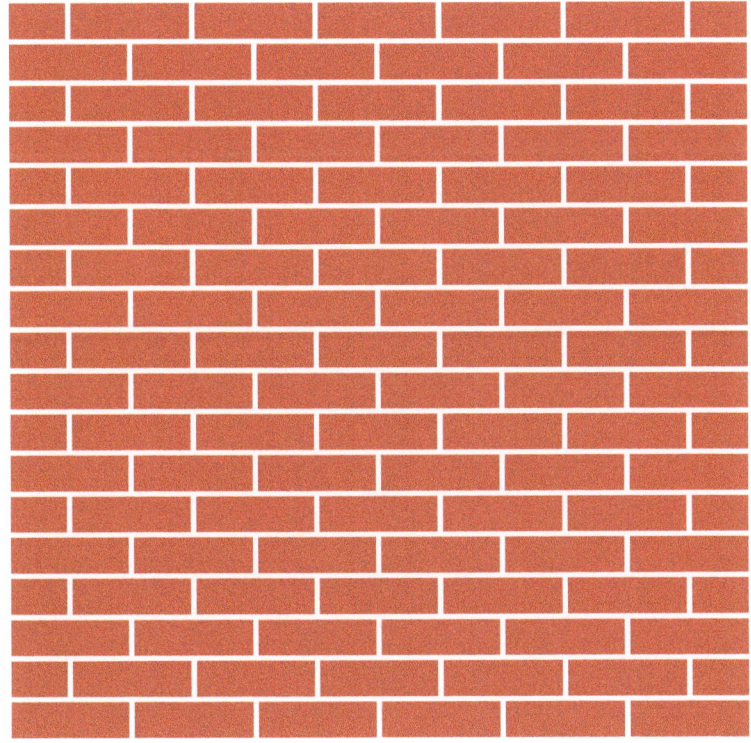

Lateral / Raked Stretcher

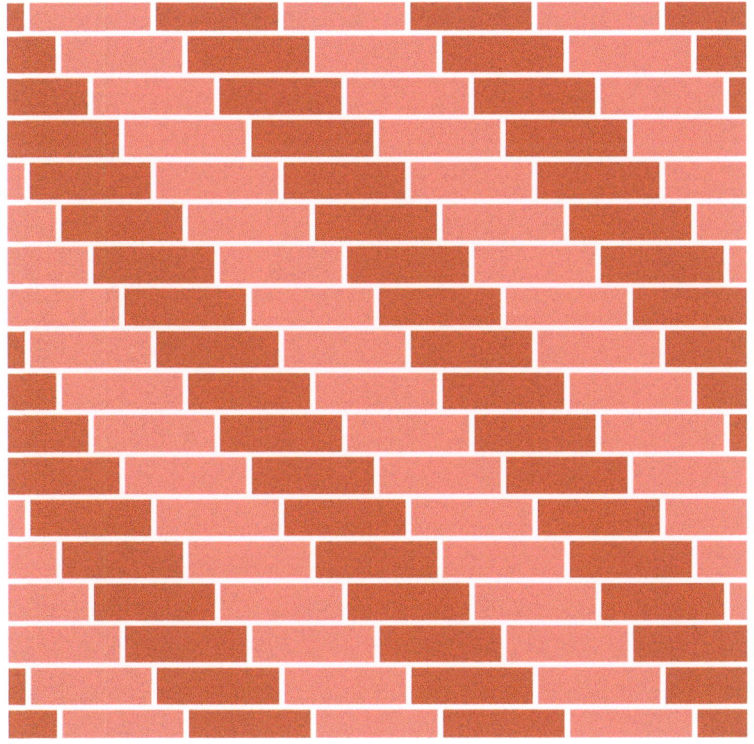

Third Staggered

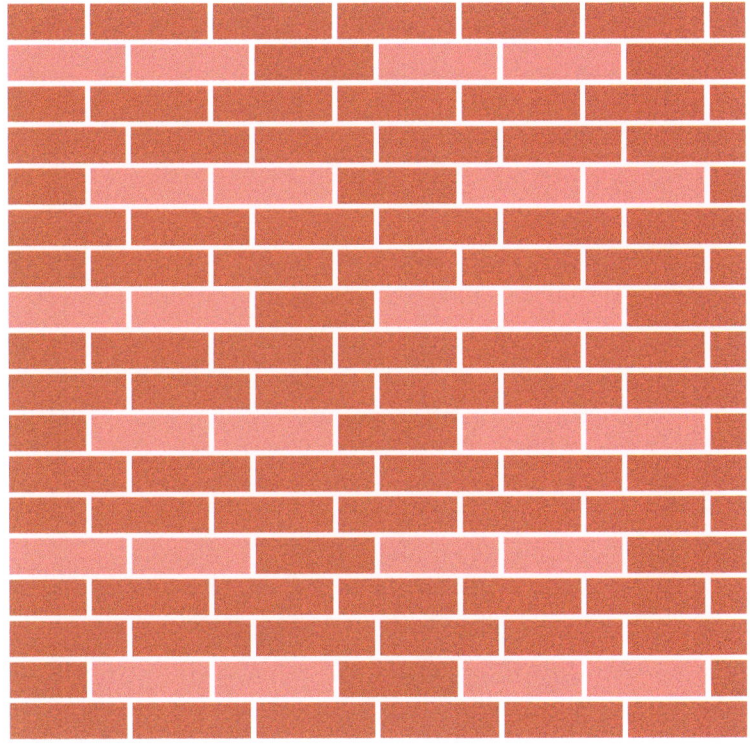

Quarter Staggered

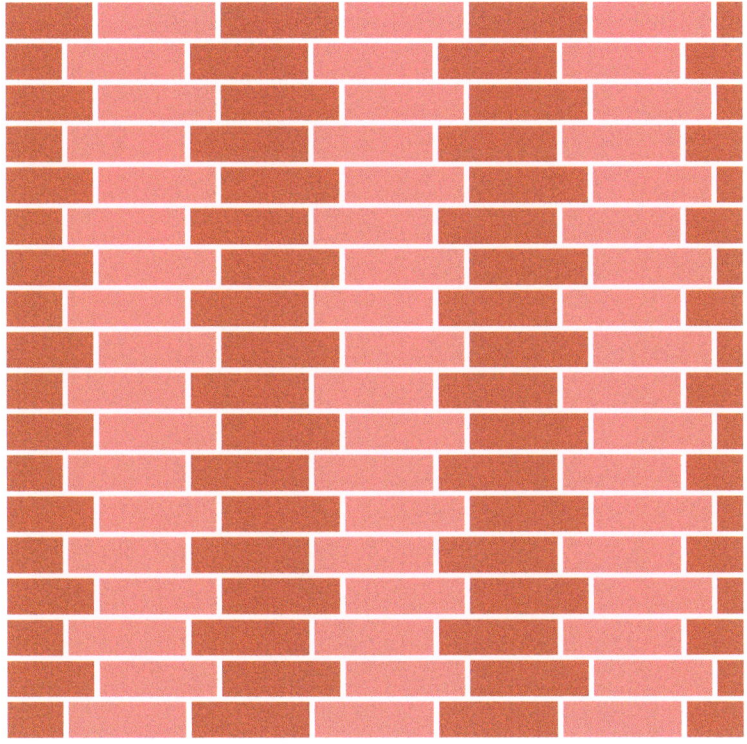

103

English Cross / Dutch

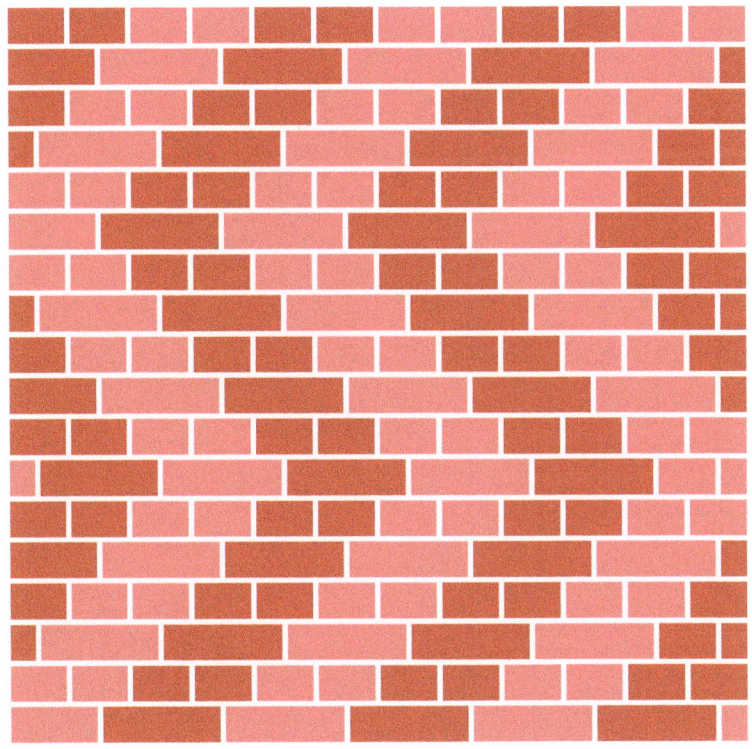

Double English Cross

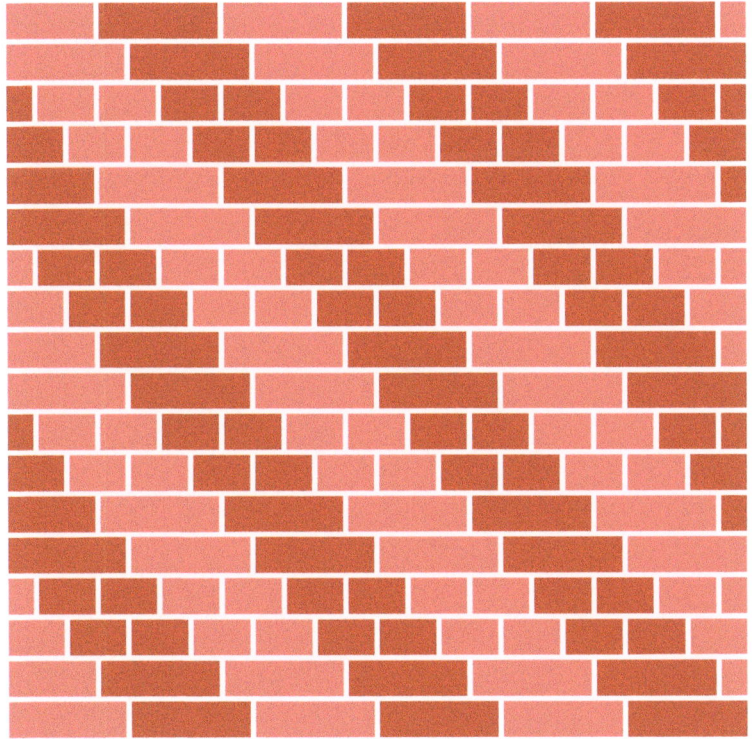

English Garden Wall

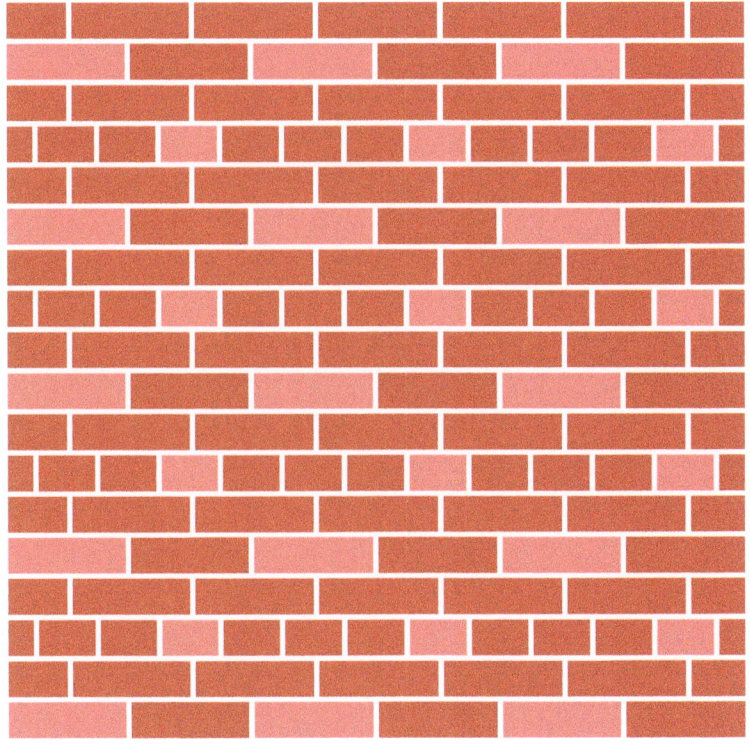

Raked English Garden Wall

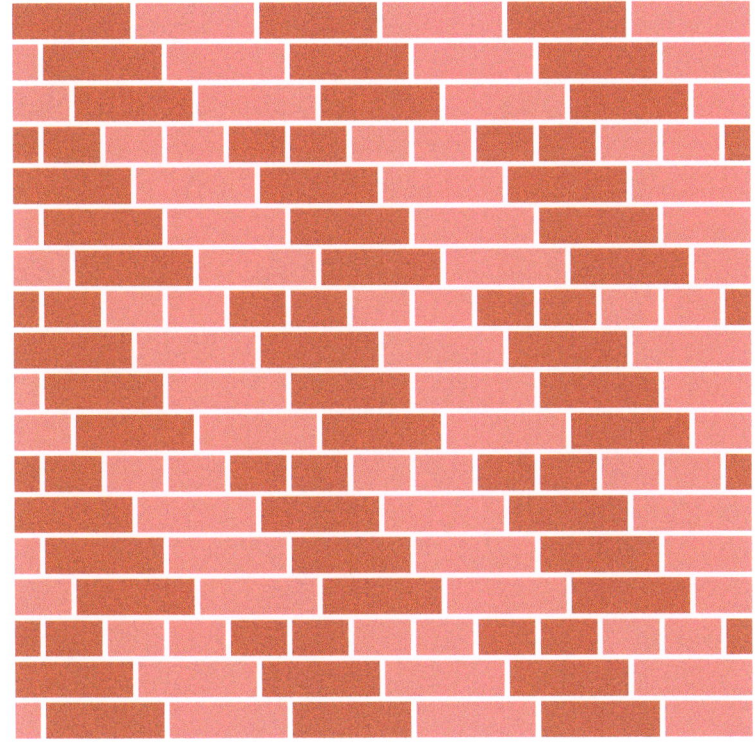

Z Dutch

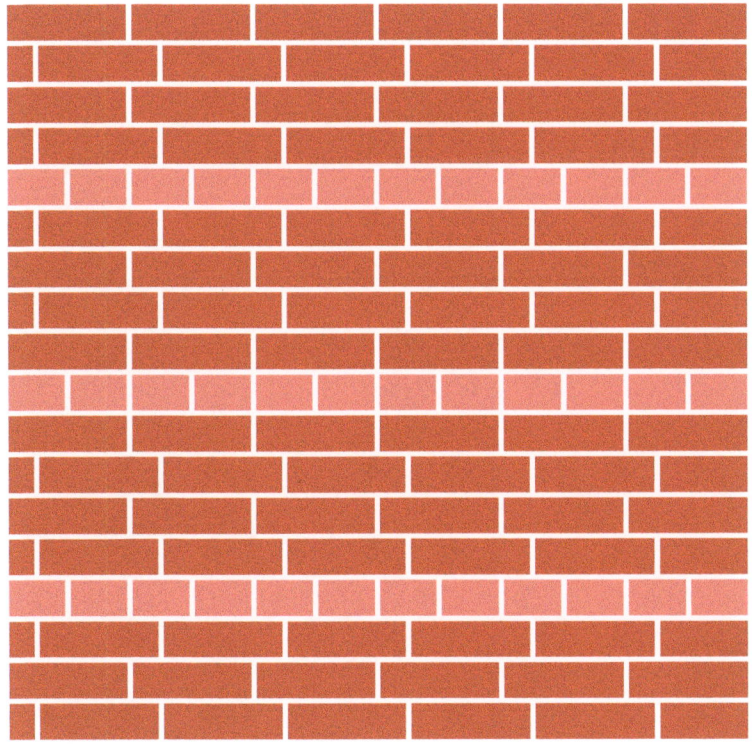

Common / American

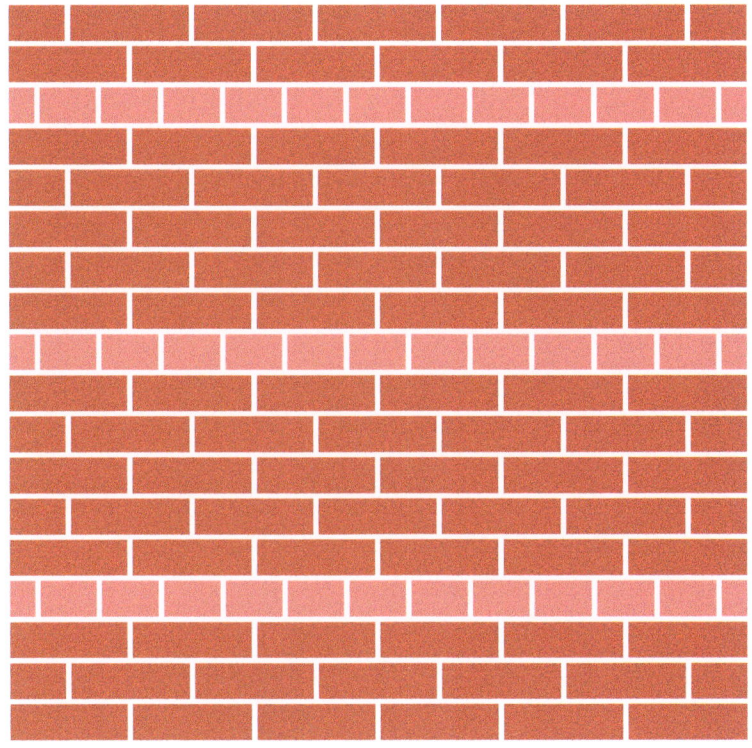

Flemish

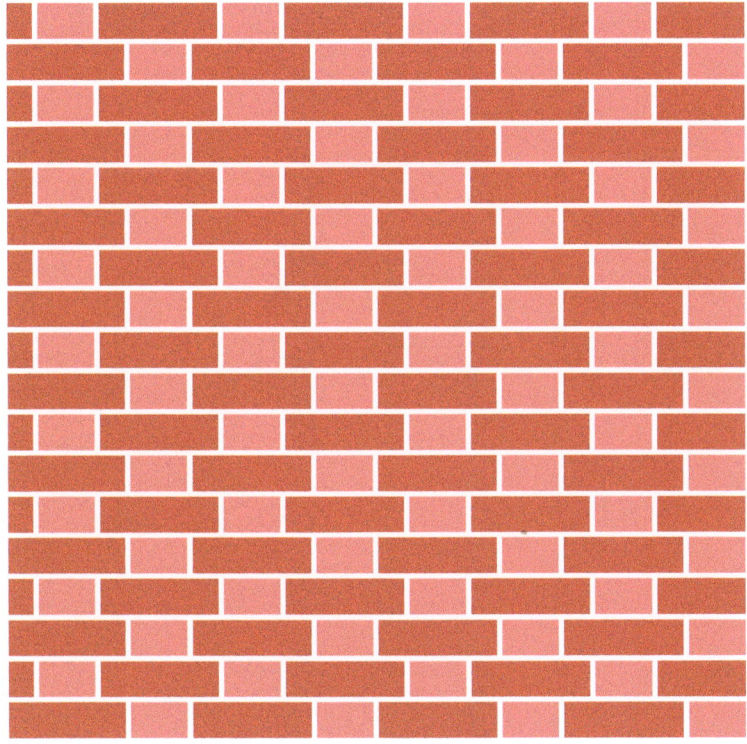

Flemish Spiral

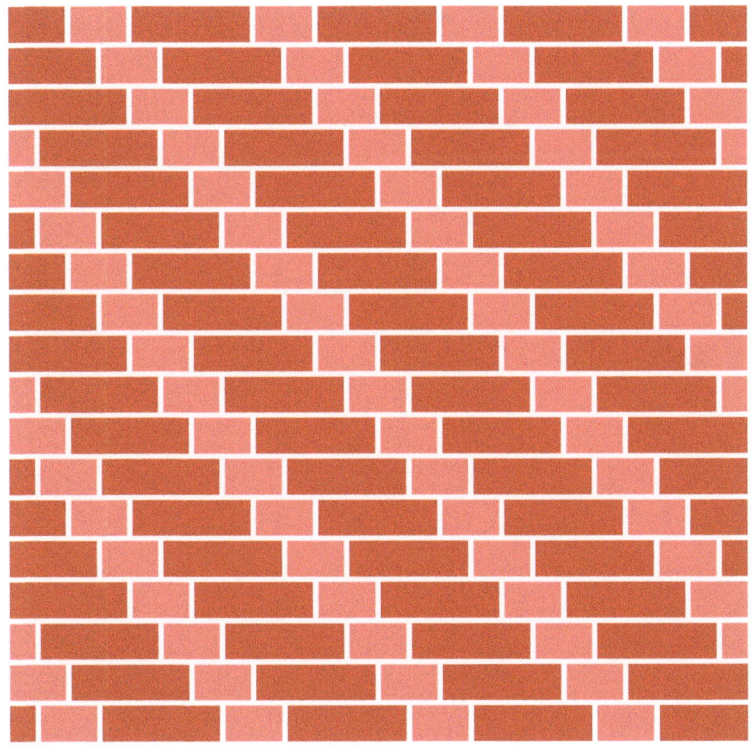

121

Gothic

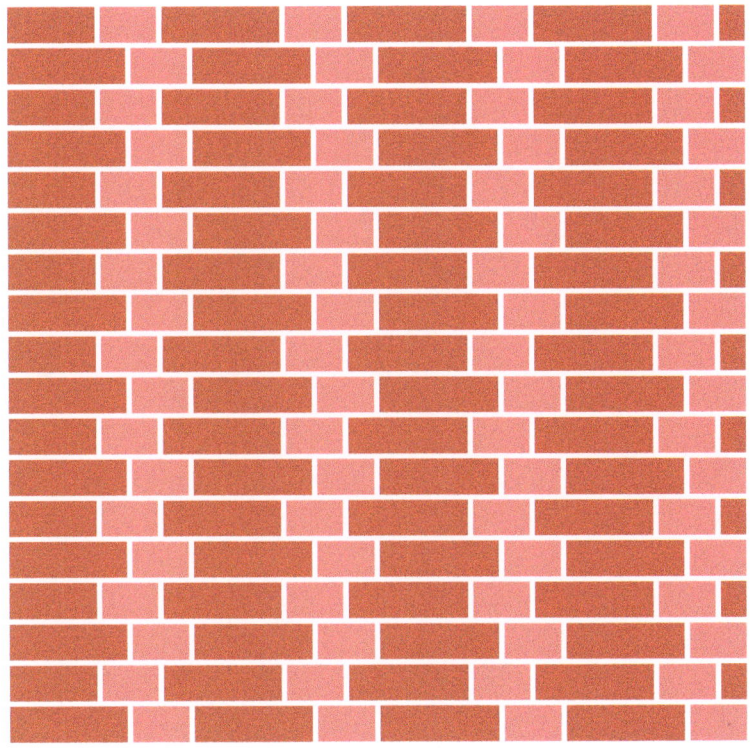

Flemish Cross

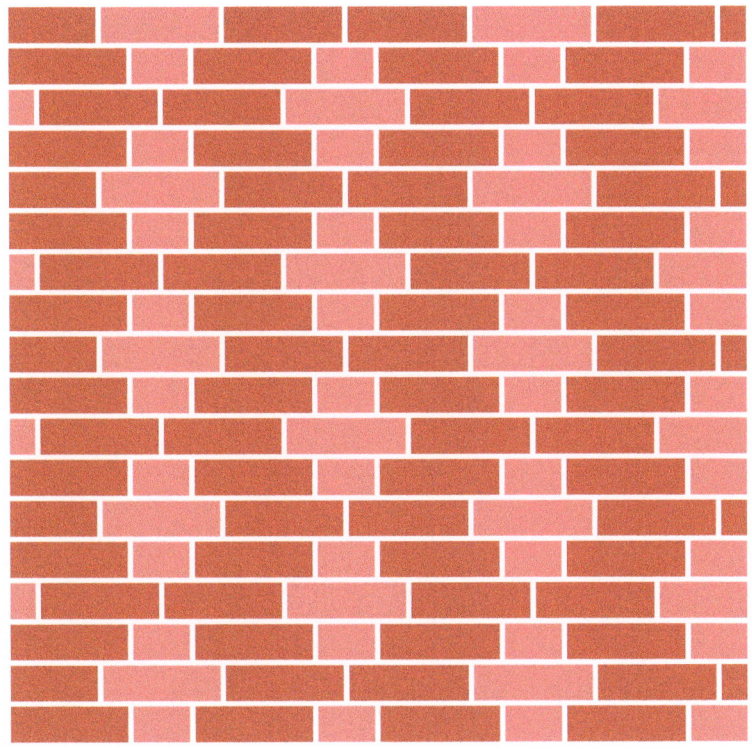

Flemish Diagonal

Double Diamond

Mixed Diamond

Zig Zag Stretcher

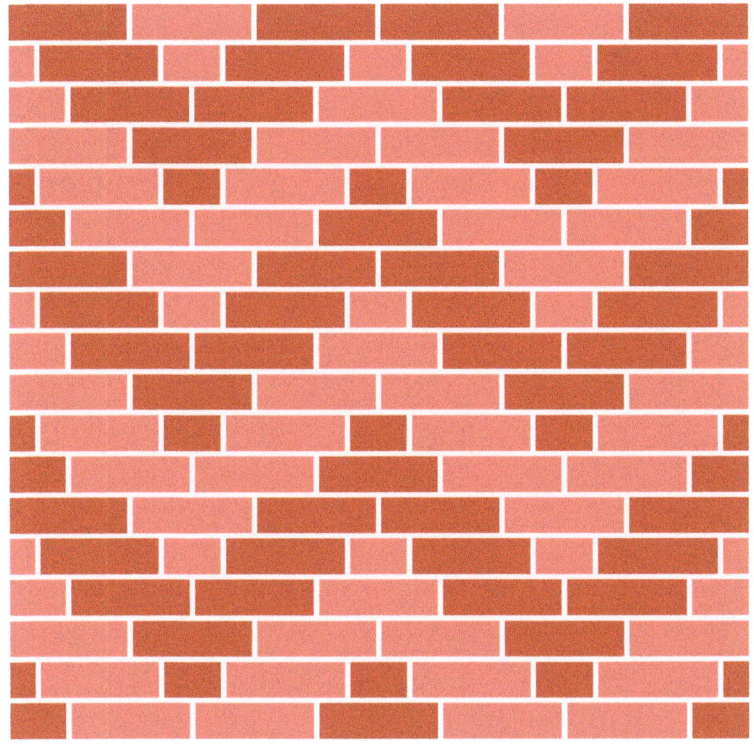

Mixed Stretcher

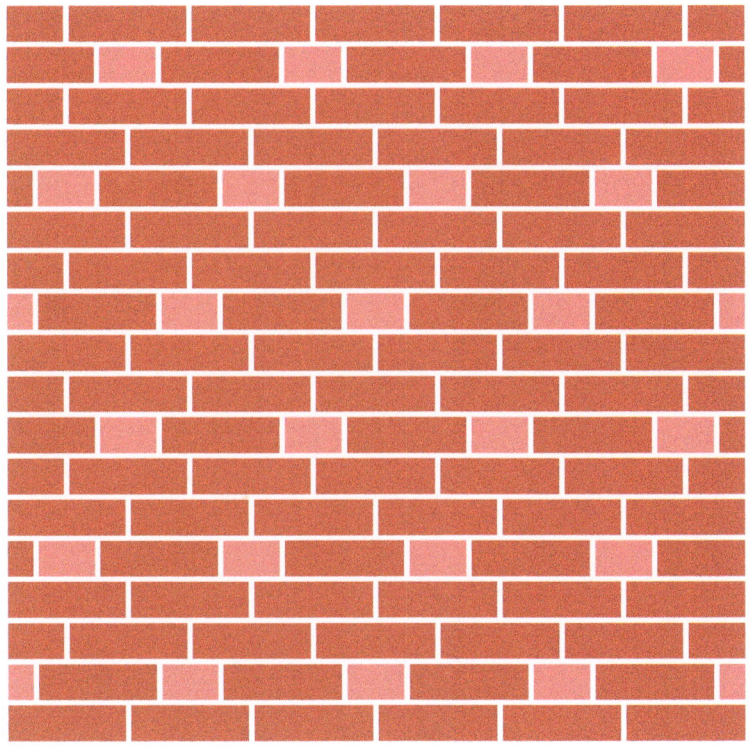

135

Flemish Stretcher

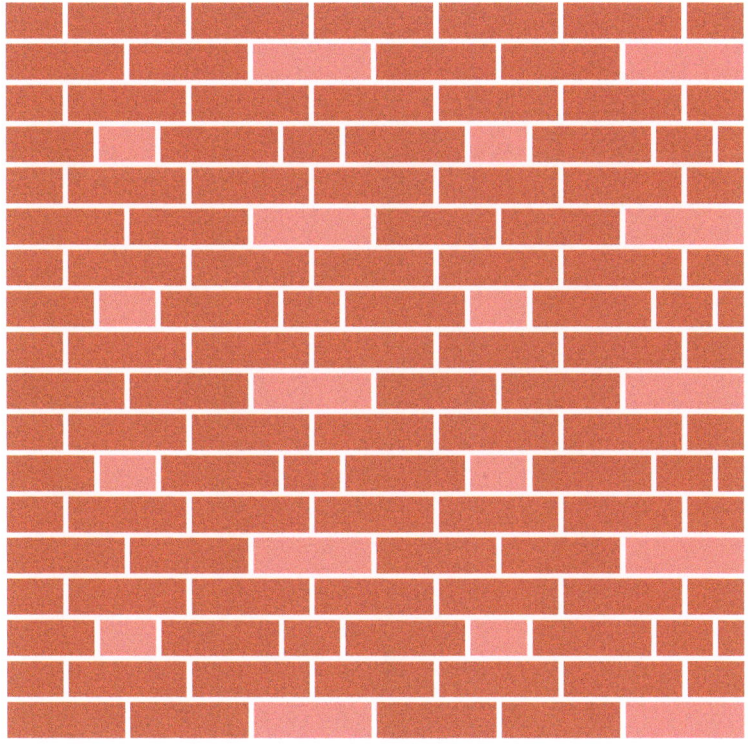

Common Flemish

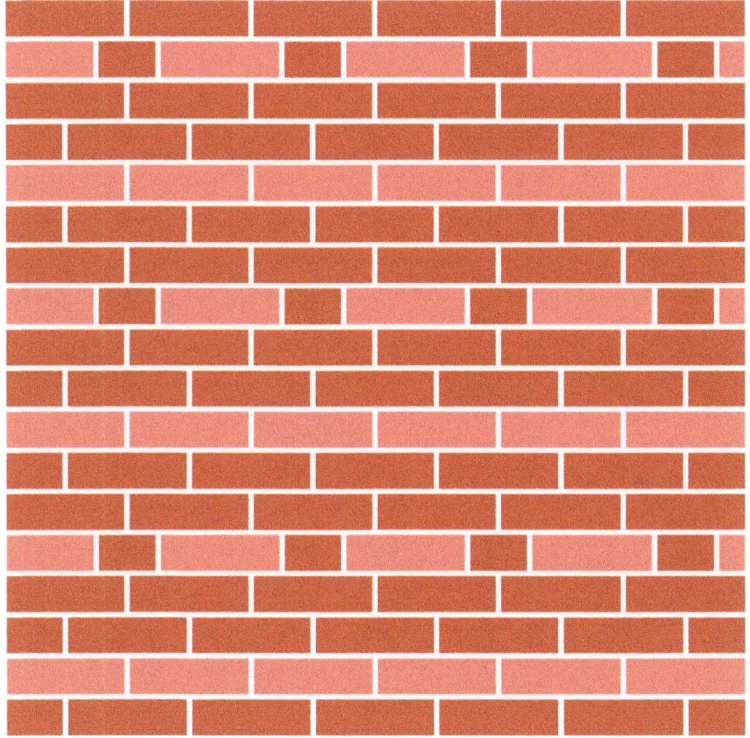

Monk / Chain / Flying / Yorkshire

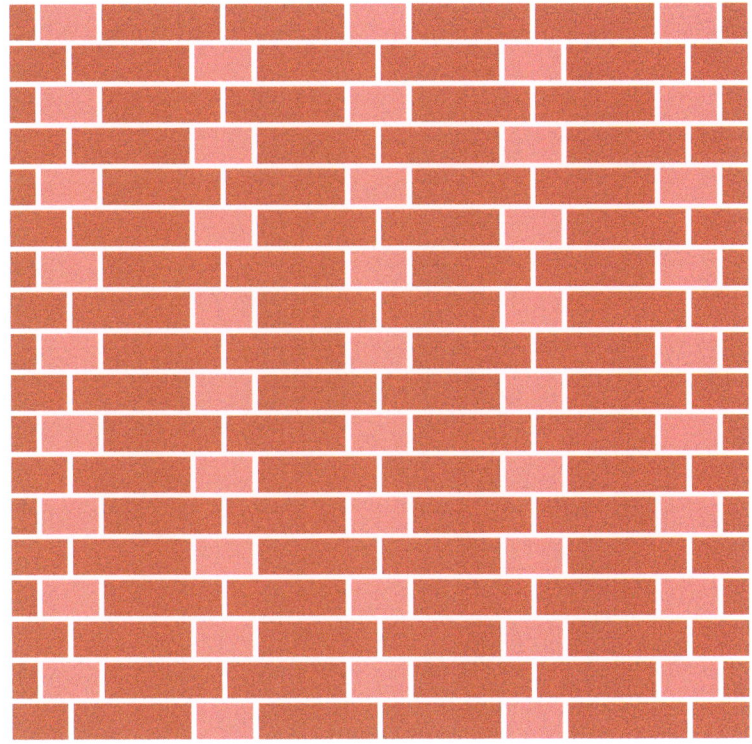

Raked Monk

143

Zig Zag Monk

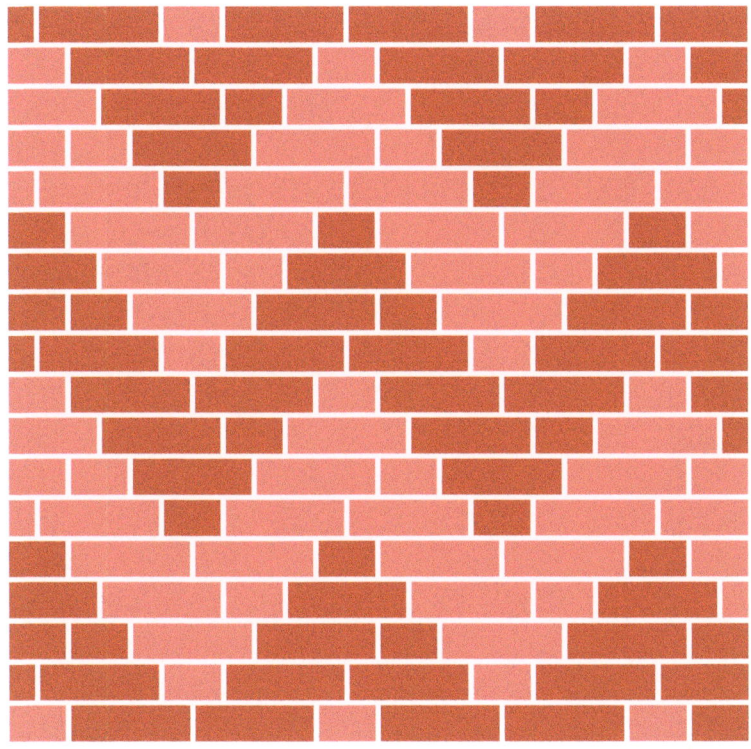

145

Stepped

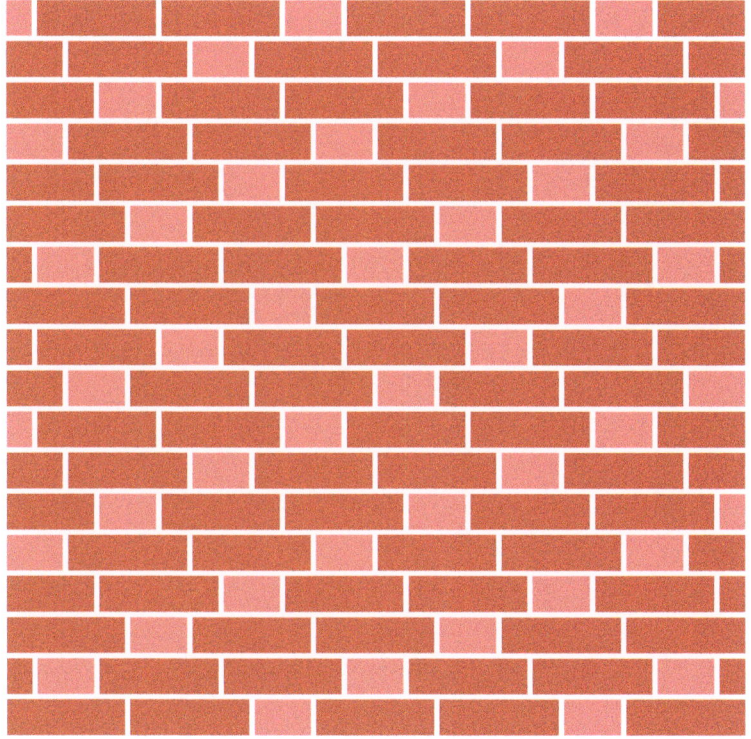

147

Silesian

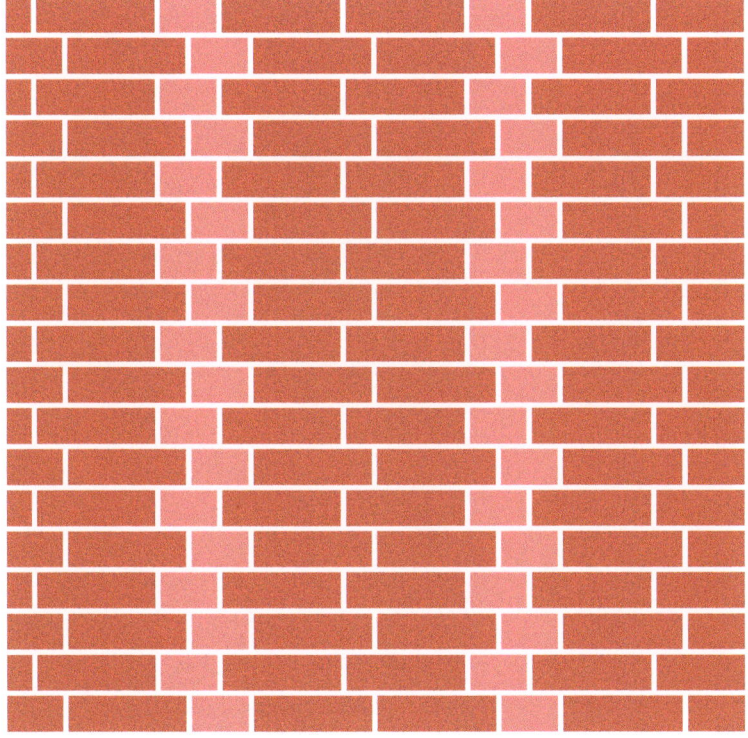

149

Modified Garden Wall

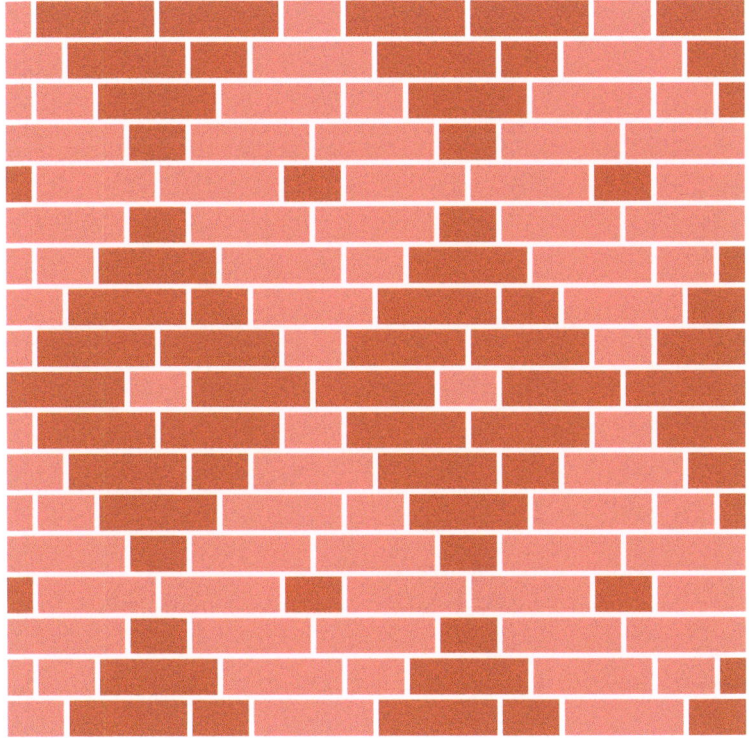

Double Stretcher Garden Wall

Flemish Garden Wall

Sussex

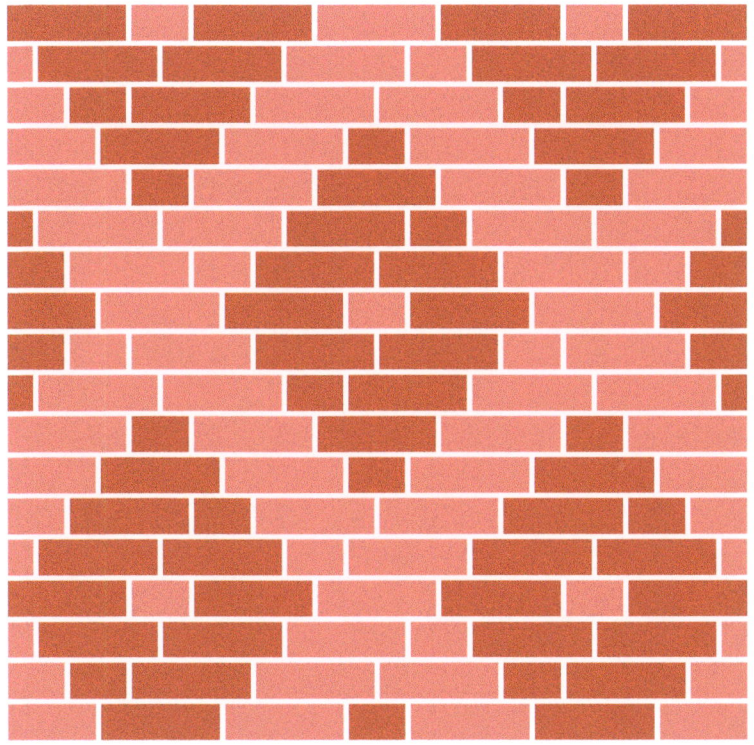

Extended Garden Wall

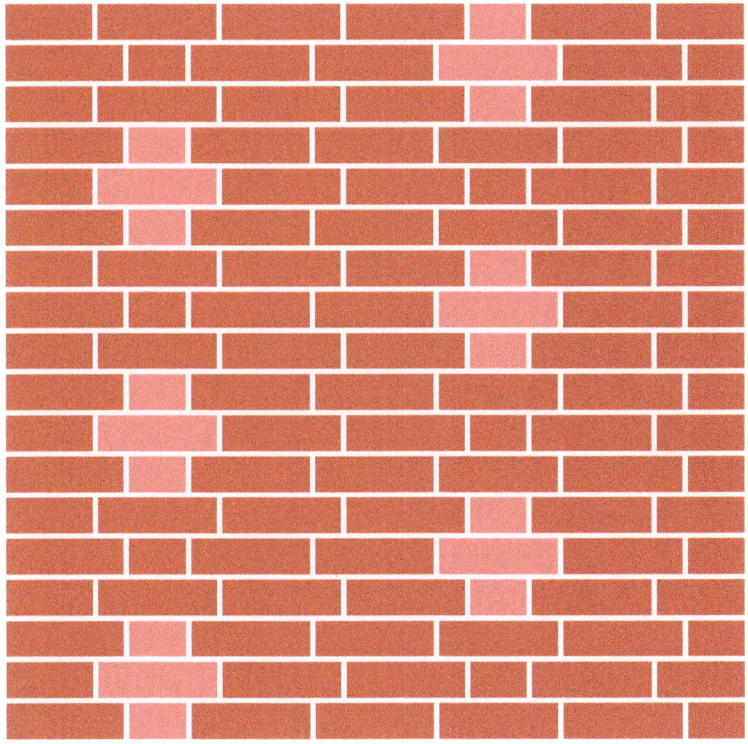

French

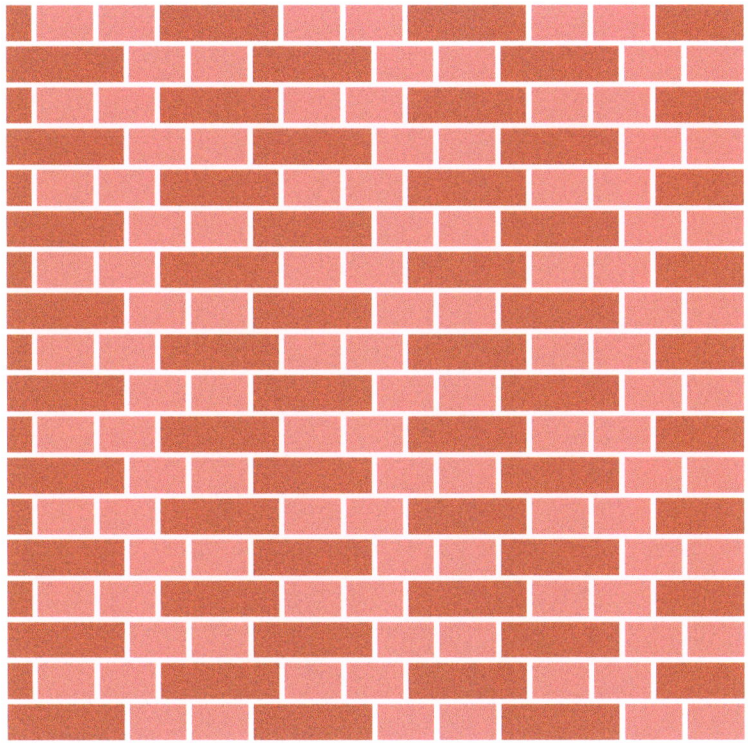

Double Flemish Cross

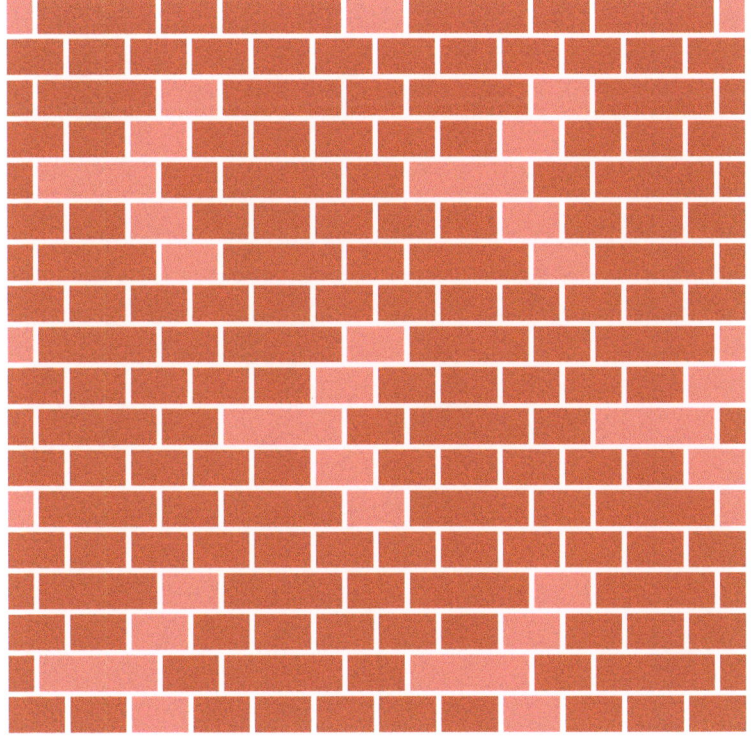

French Diamond

Diamond Header

167

Diamond Stretcher

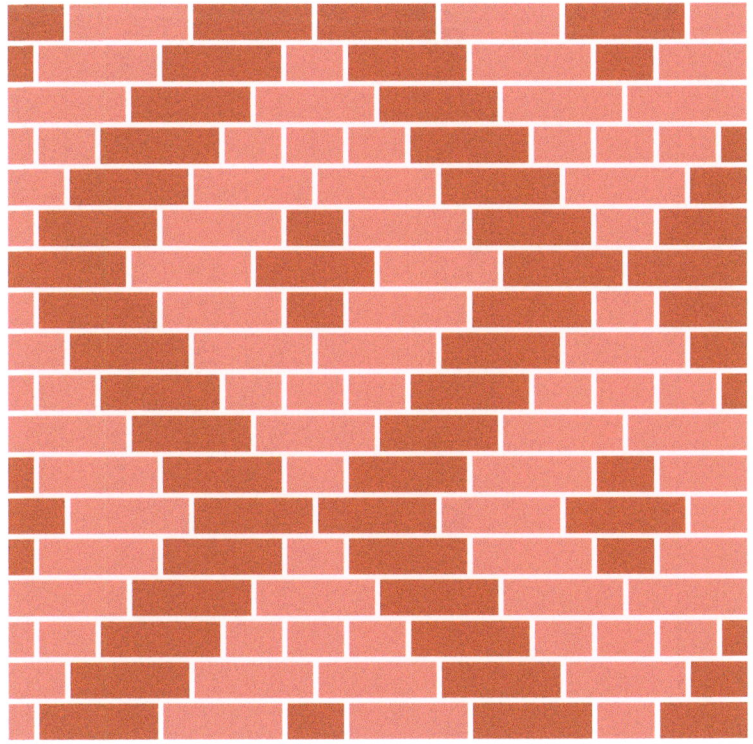

Double Diagonal

Random

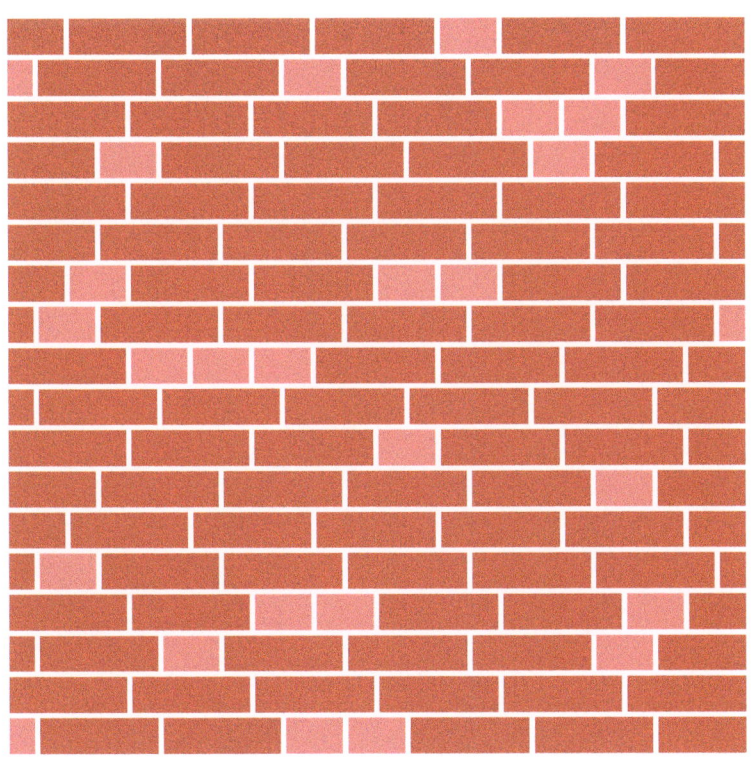

www.ingramcontent.com/pod-product-compliance
Lightning Source LLC
Chambersburg PA
CBHW051339120626
46547CB00016B/2609